Crop Circles

Crop Circles
Exploring the Designs
& Mysteries

Werner Anderhub
Hans Peter Roth

LARK BOOKS

A Division of Sterling Publishing Co.,
New York

Cover Designer: Barbara Zaretsky
Photography: All photographs by Werner Anderhub, Belp, Switzerland, unless otherwise noted.

Library of Congress Cataloging-in-Publication Data
Anderhub, Werner.
   [Geheimnis der Kornkreise. English]
   Crop circles : exploring the designs & mysteries / Werner Anderhub, Hans Peter Roth.
      p. cm.
   ISBN 1-57990-297-9
   1. Crop circles. I. Roth, Hans-Peter. II. Title.

   AG243 .A4813 2002
   001.94—dc21

                                                                2002020208

10 9 8 7 6 5 4

Published by Lark Books, a division of
Sterling Publishing Co., Inc.
387 Park Avenue South, New York, N.Y. 10016

Translation from the German: Mary Killough

English translation ©2002, Lark Books
Originally published under the title *Das Geheimnis der Kornkreise* by Werner Anderhub and Hans Peter Roth (ISBN 3-85502-694-7)
© 2000 AT Verlag, Aarau, Switzerland

Distributed in Canada by Sterling Publishing,
c/o Canadian Manda Group, One Atlantic Ave., Suite 105
Toronto, Ontario, Canada M6K 3E7

Distributed in the U.K. by Guild of Master Craftsman Publications Ltd., Castle Place, 166 High Street, Lewes, East Sussex, England BN7 1XU
Tel: (+ 44) 1273 477374, Fax: (+ 44) 1273 478606, Email: pubs@thegmcgroup.com, Web: www.gmcpublications.com

Distributed in Australia by Capricorn Link (Australia) Pty Ltd.,
P.O. Box 704, Windsor, NSW 2756 Australia

Readers should be aware that this book is translated from the original Swiss title, *Das Geheimnis der Kornkreise*. In the process of translation the editors have taken great care to preserve as much as possible the accuracy, intent, and phrasing of the original version. Because of the subtleties of language, however, no translation is a precise duplication. Readers should note, particularly, that quotations and passages from English-language sources have been re-translated and may therefore vary somewhat from the original language. Likewise, passages from foreign works available in English but originally quoted from Swiss or German versions may vary slightly from English editions.

Every effort has been made to ensure that all the information in this book is accurate. However, the publisher cannot be responsible for any injuries, losses, and other damages that may result from the use of the information in this book.

If you have questions or comments about this book, please contact:
Lark Books, 67 Broadway, Asheville, NC 28801, (828) 253-0467

Manufactured in China

For more information about Lark Books
visit our website at www.larkbooks.com

ISBN 1-57990-297-9

Table of Contents

Dedicated to the Swiss researcher, artist, and healer Emma Kunz (1892-1963).
The inestimable value of her courageous, pioneering creative work and research
will be recognized only gradually.

Preface

Just 10 years ago the concept "crop circle" was foreign to us. Then we saw the first pictures. Questions could not be suppressed. Who or what could be behind these mysterious signs? Why did they appear? How did they come about? These questions remained unanswered even after we took our first trips to southern England, the land of crop circles. Certainly we found some answers. But not *the* answer.

Years went by. And our thoughts continued to gravitate to crop circles. We both had fallen victim to the hypnotic beauty of these puzzling figures turning up year after year, always in new varieties, new shapes. The crop circles would not let us go. Subtly, our thoughts, our perceptions changed.

As far as a judgment about the "who," "how," and "why" goes, we are far from solving the riddle, unlike others who claim to have done so. For us, the saying "The more I know, the more I know that I don't know" applies. That does not mean that we remain at the very beginning of our search for answers. But it makes clear the limitations of the mind's ability to fully understand the world around us and in us.

Whatever is incomplete strives for completion; astonishment and reverence are concepts that take us to new horizons. We may say of our own experience that, no matter what their origin, crop circles have awakened anew in us an astonishment and reverence for this limitless world. If this book can inspire and motivate a few people, if it can demonstrate to them by means of crop circles how wonderful life and creation are, then it has more than fulfilled its purpose.

Children have not closed their eyes to the mystery of life and its discovery. They show this to adults by their inquisitive behavior every day. Crop circles can help us to remember that one of the greatest gifts our children possess is the ability to be amazed, to wonder, to ask questions honestly and to remain open to answers.

Bern, November 2001
Hans Peter Roth and Werner Anderhub

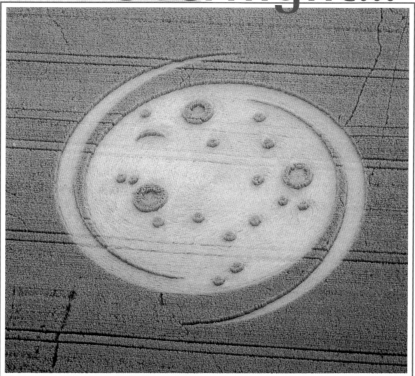

I It Happened
Overnight...

The Discovery

"Nothing." Andreas lowers the night scope. He remains silent for a moment and looks in the direction of the wheat field as if his eyes could penetrate the hazy darkness better than the infrared device. A gigantic grain field, the "East Field," sprawls for over half a mile along the left side of the rural road between Alton Barnes and Pewsey.

Year after year crop circle formations have shown up here; among them are several of the most puzzling and complicated. In 1999 two figures were discovered at the same time on a June morning. One of them stretches out over 374 yards (340 m) in perfect geometric form (Ill. 1). Not far from that a snake almost 187 yards (170 m) long, with nine coils, appears to wind its way through the field (Ill. 136). Both formations can still be easily recognized. But over the course of weeks they were trampled on badly by curious people and have been altered too by wind, rain, and growth of the grain. They only vaguely resemble their original condition. Still, people come. Because "it has happened" in East Field before, attention is directed more closely to this and other fields

 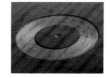

Ill. 1

Ill. 1: "The Medley," East Field, Alton Barnes, July 12, 1999, 374 yards (340 m), barley

Ill. 2: "The Ring," earthen wall of Avebury, August 2, 1998, 109 yards (99 m), wheat

Ill. 3: "Fractal," Silbury Hill, July 24, 1999

where crop circles frequently have been found.

No breath of air disturbs the stalks of grain wet with dew. The mist shimmers silvery blue over the fields under the deep crescent moon and seems to swallow every sound. The gravel crunches beneath footsteps. The sound of the car's engine starting disrupts the silence. Like glowing fingers the headlights feel their way through several layers of fog toward Avebury Ring, one of the earthen wall sites interspersed with a gigantic circle of stones, part of this very large prehistoric monument in England. A long row of menhirs, as the gigantic standing stones are called, shows the way. Timidly, the first pale hint of dawn reaches into the darkness and mixes with the moonlight.

It is shortly after 4 A.M. The little hamlet of Avebury lies sleeping. A few sheep bleat in the distance. The first birds greet the morning more wide awake than the neo-Druid, clad in a brown robe similar to a monk's habit, who calls out to the passing vehicle. "Emenon," he says, gesturing sleepily toward the east. Shivering, he immediately shuffles back to his place of sleep.

The circular path on the grass-covered earthen wall at Avebury allows a view of a beautiful field off to the northeast. Here as well, early risers in recent years have been surprised now and then by new formations in the grain (Ill. 2). It is still too dark to be able to make out the contours. The high-pitched humming of the night scope is becoming familiar. "Nothing here either," Andreas states laconically. The morning sky gradually begins to gain color in the east. It is bitterly cold.

The car doors bang shut. Now the car heads in the direction of the small town of Devizes. Barely a half mile (1 km) away from Avebury lies Silbury Hill, a powerful 132-foot-high (40 m) earthen hill, piled layer upon layer by human hands millennia ago. The conical structure with its flattened tip is considered the largest pyramid in Europe (Ill. 3). In the immediate vicinity there are five crop circles. Most of them would be easily visible from the earthen pyramid, but it is forbidden to climb on it. As the car passes the hill its heater spreads a welcome, sleep-inducing warmth among the little group of observers, up since 3 A.M. Day breaks with hardly a cloud in the sky. The eastern horizon begins to light up in strong red-orange pastel colors.

Shortly before entering the city of Devizes the car turns sharply to the right into a small lane. Now the way is getting narrow. On both sides are embankments covered in hedges. It would be impossible for an oncoming car to pass. On the right, Roundway Hill Farm comes into view. Gently, then more and more steeply, the little lane

Ill. 3

11

climbs several hundred yards to the farm-stead. Our next destination, Roundway Hill, is in sight. It offers an excellent vantage point of the surrounding fields. On the right, below the road, a gigantic wheat field meas-uring almost 75 acres (30 ha) looms like a phantom against the backdrop of dawn. Andreas puts away his night scope. The morning light is sufficient now to survey the fields with the naked eye. He throws an ini-tial, casual, inquiring glance at the grain fields out the window of the moving car. Outlines of shadows in the sea of grain appear approximately 330 yards (300 m) from the lane not far from a high-tension wire, which runs across the field. The young German squints. The rest of the group has detected something as well. The vehicle is quickly parked in an opening in the lane. Andreas rubs his eyes in wonder. Maybe wind damage? But otherwise the entire field appears to be intact. The shadows are con-centrated in a clearly defined area and exhibit a certain regularity.

A look through binoculars confirms it: the structures differ from the rest of the field too clearly and systematically to stem from some natural cause. And the group agrees that what they have discovered just now was not present in the grain yesterday. Morning after morning they have visited the field at the foot of Roundway Hill, as well as other fields where impressive crop circle for-mations have been discovered previously. This formation is new.

From this flat perspective exact forms can-not be discerned, but it is definitely a geomet-ric figure of gigantic proportions (Ill. 4).

Ill. 4

An almost familiar mixture of joy, excite-ment, recognition, and amazement is felt. It has happened again—and, again, during the night. This giant something, this figure, can be distinguished against the daylight as it grows brighter, as if it had always lain there—like an enormous stamp that belongs to this landscape.

The next step is clear: ask the farmer of Roundway Hill Farm for permission to enter this field to examine the crop circle forma-tion. Christopher Combe is surprised. This farmer, who has leased almost 1.2 square miles (3 km2) from Her Majesty the queen, has no knowledge of the formation. He comes along himself to the field and shakes his head when he sees the immense area of low-lying grain. Yet he remains quiet and astonishingly calm and casual. The little

Ill. 5

III. 6

group follows a "tramline," as the rutted tracks the farmers drive their tractors along to spray their fields are called, and reaches the formation.

The surface of the flattened wheat stalks is so large that at first it is almost impossible to take it in at one glance and discern the geometric pattern. This figure is 137.5 yards (125 m) in diameter. That is determined by a preliminary rough measurement. After the pictogram has been paced off, its form gradually becomes clear. A gigantic inner circle, regular in shape, is surrounded in turns by seven larger and seven smaller points. The end of each of the 14 "points" is closed off by a larger or smaller circle. However, the most puzzling thing is the way in which the grain stalks in this crown-shaped pictogram have been flattened. They too follow geometric patterns and follow the outlines of the figure far into the large inner circle. No corners. No overlapping. Everything is laid out in soft, flowing forms, "as though poured out in one single molten mass, which has suddenly solidified," observes Andreas (Ills. 6, 8, 10).

The first gleaming rays of the rising summer sun intensify this impression. Depending on the direction of their stalks, many of the little spears of ripe grain glitter like gold. Chris Combe struggles for words: "At first I thought this was a nighttime prank. But now I cannot imagine how such a complex and gigantic figure could be produced in my field in a single night without anyone noticing." A rough estimate is that more than 7,200 square yards (6000 m²) of Combe's grain is shaped into this figure. The farmer is drawn to one part, then another of the huge design. "This formation was not here yesterday evening—I know, because I was working in an adjoining field. If it was created by

13

III. 7

something other than human hands, I'm actually proud of that fact, that something like this has happened in my field, of all places." For that reason he would have no objections, he says when asked, to investigators conducting further research on "his" formation. "For a couple of nice aerial photos in return," he replies, laughing and gesturing toward the morning sky. The ripening grain crackles under his shoes as he makes his way with heavy steps back to his tractor.

The little plane's motor starts with a roar (III. 5). After only 110 yards (100 m) over a bumpy, grassy slope the ultralight airplane is in the air, lifting off from Clench Common. Graham Slater guides his craft steeply into the bright blue, nearly windless morning sky. A few hundred yards beneath the little plane the hedge-bordered landscape, typical of old England and amazingly still intact, spreads out below, interspersed with large willows and fields of rape and corn. The nose of the high-winged ultralight is pointing toward the northwest. The flight in the direction of Devizes goes over the little village of Marlborough, where the legendary master Merlin from the story of the Holy Grail is supposedly buried.

III. 7: "Six-pointed Star" at the dolmen of Devil's Den near Marlborough

III. 8: "The Crown," Roundway, Devizes, July 31, 1999, 137.5 yards (125 m), wheat

A few miles farther west of "Merlinborough," the first figure becomes visible. Executed with unbelievable precision, a star with six points lies sharply engraved in the field of grain, which is still green (Ill. 7; see also Ills. 142-144). Only 33 yards (30 m) from this lies the "Devil's Den," where an ancient stone monument, a type called a dolmen, stands. A rock weighing tons lies across two massive stone supports; it is similar to numerous other such structures in southern England. The somewhat isolated depression surrounded by hedges, within which the dolmen and crop circle formation lie, lend the entire panorama enchanting beauty.

There are still about 10 miles to fly until the plane reaches Roundway Hill near Devizes. But several miles before this destination the massive crop circle formation at Roundway Hill Farm is already clearly visible. Four minutes later Graham Slater begins to circle above "The Crown" in steep swooping flight patterns. The newest crop circle was given this nickname only a few hours earlier, soon after it was discovered. Pointing steeply downward, the plane flies in tight circles, its right wing banked sharply toward the formation. The sight from this height—about 990 feet (300 m)—is overwhelming; the formation is gigantic (Ill. 8).

And what you could only imagine from the ground becomes a certainty from a bird's-eye view: not only the outline of the figure appears absolutely precise and geometrically perfect. So, too, is the arrangement of the flattened grain within the formation. Because it glistens in the morning sun in various shadings, according to the direction you see it from, the crop circle has a stunning three-dimensional character. It is as though an immense piece of gold jewelry, such as a brooch, is lying in the countryside.

After circling above Roundway Hill for a while, Graham Slater guides the plane in the direction of Avebury, first taking a small detour toward Cherhill. There in the grain field at the foot of the rather steep Oldbury Castle Hill lies another crop circle, just two weeks old. It too is among the most beautiful discovered this summer. Six crescent moons are lying clockwise, one within the

Ill. 9

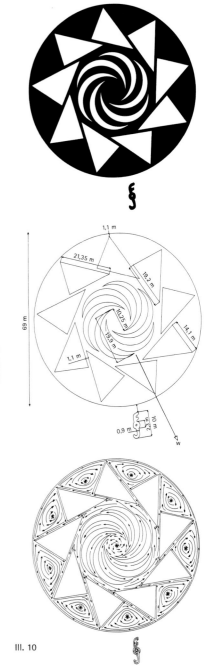

Ill. 9: "Nine-pointed Star," Cherhill with white horse, July 18, 1999, 88 yards (80 m), wheat

Ill. 10: Diagram of "Nine-pointed Star" (drawn by Andreas Müller)

Ill. 11: "Galaxy," West Stowell, near Pewsey, July 23, 1994, 71.5 yards (65 m)

Ill. 10

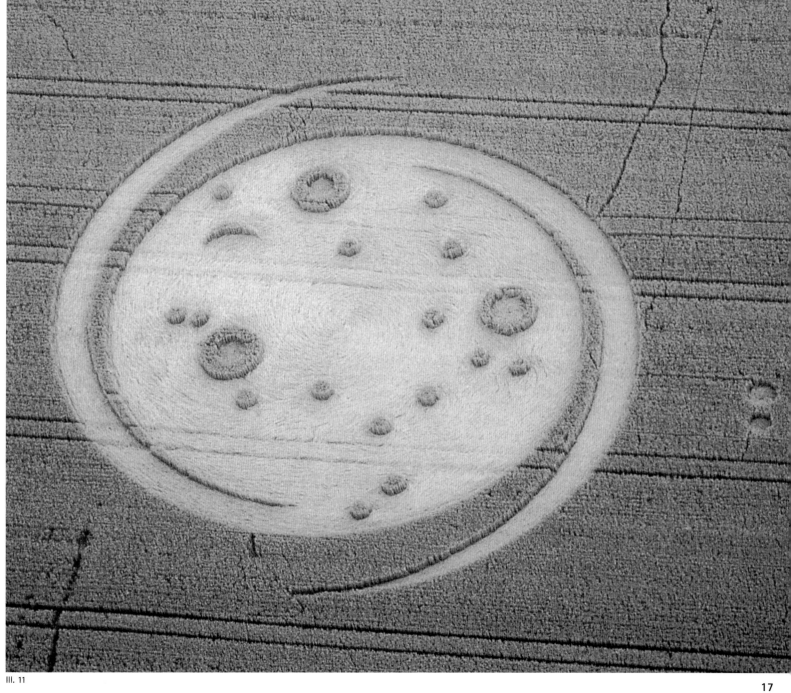

III. 11

other. A star consisting of nine triangles surrounds the "Crescent Moon Windmill." The entire figure lies within a circle about 88 yards (80 m) in diameter (Ill. 9).

Graham Slater was first asked by people interested in crop circles for flights above Wiltshire County in 1996. Because passenger flights in conventional small planes were becoming increasingly expensive and were prevented in part by the British Transport Ministry because of licensing regulations, more and more people switched to ultralight planes for taking photos of crop circles. Slater says he was somewhat "astonished and turned off by this new fuss about these crop circles." He had known of the phenomenon but had hardly been interested in it up to that time. "But now it has gotten to me as well," he admits. "The sheer size and beauty of these figures seen from the sky is so surprising and impressive, now I find myself waiting for each new crop circle season with great anticipation." Despite the ultralight's relatively limited range, on today's flights above Wiltshire County enthusiastic passengers can admire close to 20 formations, including several of the season's most beautiful. After an hour the pilot lands his machine safely on the grass again at Clench Common.

The campground at Alton Barnes seems dead. Several houseboats are anchored lazily in the brown water of the Kennet-Avon Canal in front of the Barge Inn. Many visitors at the pub and adjacent campground have gone immediately to Roundway Hill after they learned about the new crop circle

Ill. 12

formation there, "The Crown." Since this area has become the worldwide focal point of the crop circle phenomenon, the Barge Inn can . no longer be compared to other pubs and campgrounds in the sleepy, rural environment of Wiltshire County. When the first very large, complex crop circle figures appeared in nearby East Field at the beginning of the 1990s, the Barge Inn became *the* meeting place for people interested in the phenomenon.

The "croppies" (as people interested in crop circles are called, either fondly or with a touch of mild humor) gather in the billiard room behind the bar, with its wonderfully painted ceiling. Here they exchange the latest information about freshly formed crop circles in the vicinity, as well as in all of South England and worldwide. The locations of crop circles from former years are marked in red or orange on a regional map; those that have turned up this year are marked in green. Aerial photos of many of the formations are attached. Day and night the "croppies" discuss the what, when, where, how, who, and why of the crop circles.

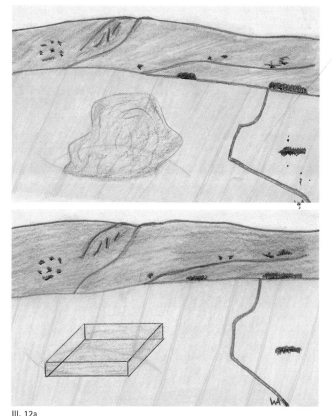

III. 12a

nity for taking good aerial photos. The gleam of the low-lying stalks dances warm and golden, contrasting with the lengthening shadows. Several ultralight planes take turns circling above "The Crown" on Roundway Hill. Even Andreas has returned to the majestic formation, which lies scarcely 6 miles (10 km) from the Barge Inn. In the remaining two hours of sufficient daylight, the German crop circle researcher wants to measure "The Crown" exactly. His purpose is to to produce as detailed a sketch as possible, one showing the exact direction of the flattened stalks—whether clockwise or counterclockwise—as well as the figure's geometric construction, and more (III. 10).

As twilight approaches he is finishing his work. The pleasant coolness that has crept into the field after sunset becomes chillier, and a soft wind rises. The time has come to leave the place. Already the first stars glitter timidly. The chirping of the crickets is soothing but at the same time creates a tension. What further surprises will the darkness settling over Wiltshire, the moonless sky dotted with shining stars, bring?

Lights above the Field

Actually we should have been in the field sooner on this unusual night in August, 1994. But a violent evening thunderstorm, without rain but with all the more impressive light and sound against the backdrop of Wiltshire, detains us from an early departure. Only toward 11:30 P.M. do we finally reach the remote field at the sleepy hamlet of West Stowell. The destination of our night-

time excursion, the crop circle named "Galaxy," appeared a few days earlier and lies 165 yards (150 m) ahead, invisible in the darkness (III. 11). Word had gotten around long ago that the flat area at the foot of Golden Ball Hill (III. 12) was not only a place where crop circles frequently appeared, but was also where people had repeatedly been confronted with strange appearances of light.

Many stars sparkle above. The ghostly blue-green storm clouds gradually begin disappearing. Still, the two of us cannot get rid of a slight feeling of uneasiness. It had begun with an incident an hour ago, upon leaving the Barge Inn pub: Suddenly, above the roof of the building, for only a moment, we saw something that still seems to us an absurd optical illusion. It was as though a flying full moon, inserted for a short time as if in a film, raced over the roof. Was it perhaps a shooting star? No. It was too large. And it was flying in a horizontal but slightly upward direction.

We are about to enter the field on the tractor path when something incomprehensible happens. And yet, it is no illusion. Both of us see clearly and plainly a bright, blue-white light beginning to manifest itself as though it is coming directly out of the interior of the crop circle. Something like a cloud takes shape in front of us and hovers above the crop circle a short time, illuminating the remote stretch of land lying around us. Then the body of light moves toward the sky and dissolves like a swath of fog.

With pounding pulses, unmoving and speechless, we stand tensely in the darkness

It is pleasantly cool in the pub. Outside, however, the sun is scorching the last moisture from earth already rent with dry furrows. The summer of 1999, like others in the 1990s in Wiltshire, has been extremely dry and hot. People who are up at 3 in the morning and seldom land in bed before 11 P.M. like to take a siesta during the hottest hours of the day.

Toward evening, however, the temperatures are more bearable even in the blazing sun. On clear days it is a wonderful opportu-

as what we experienced is repeated. Over a period of several minutes we witness three similar sequences of events (Ill. 12a, top). During the fourth repetition the most puzzling thing happens: within a few seconds after the source of light rises up again from the crop circle, cloudlike, it changes immediately into a three-dimensional rectangular form of enormous size (Ill. 12a, bottom). Now the blue-white light appears to be bundled into a shoebox-shaped body of approximately 6.5 x 22 x 55 yards (6 x 20 x 50 m), shimmering transparently like a jellyfish and floating several feet above the "Galaxy."

Suddenly this rectangle of light begins to move toward us. Remaining at the edge of the field becomes a test of nerves—and my companion can no longer stand it. He expresses fear and wants to leave. To our surprise the geometric figure of light stops moving forward and floats back over the crop circle, then changes back into cloud form and dissipates, rising toward the sky. In the darkness that now surrounds us again, we are joined by two other people who, earlier at the pub, had agreed to meet us at the crop circle. Both of them notice our agitation. What can we say to them? We try to describe the geometric figure. But what we have just witnessed is completely beyond the limits of human experience. Then, as the source of light is again manifested to all four of us in a way similar to the first three sequences, the newcomers realize that something very important has taken place.

After puzzling over this and discussing it for a while, we all walk to the crop circle's interior. The mood in this secluded spot is now peaceful. The two people who joined us leave. As we prepare to leave also, something else very strange occurs: for a moment our hearts flutter. We look at each other questioningly, then both nod with unspoken understanding. It is as though something needed to be settled back into place in our hearts.

Looking back, we can talk about all this very soberly. But taken in context it was a very startling experience that enlarged our worldview permanently. Even though it cannot be explained rationally, it set many things in motion for us. Reverence and amazement were indelibly and unforgettably impressed within us that night.

We must stress: we did not witness the emergence of a new crop circle but, rather, experienced an event at an existing circle. Neither in the literature nor in conversations with others could a similar description be found. At lectures the same question always arises: Why didn't it occur to one of us to make a video or photograph of the event, since it lasted several minutes? Our counter questions would be: "In a similar situation would you have the presence of mind to film it? Would it be possible even to capture on film what happened?" We describe this nighttime sighting neither to convince others of our experience nor to prove something with it.

II History Goes 'Round in Circles

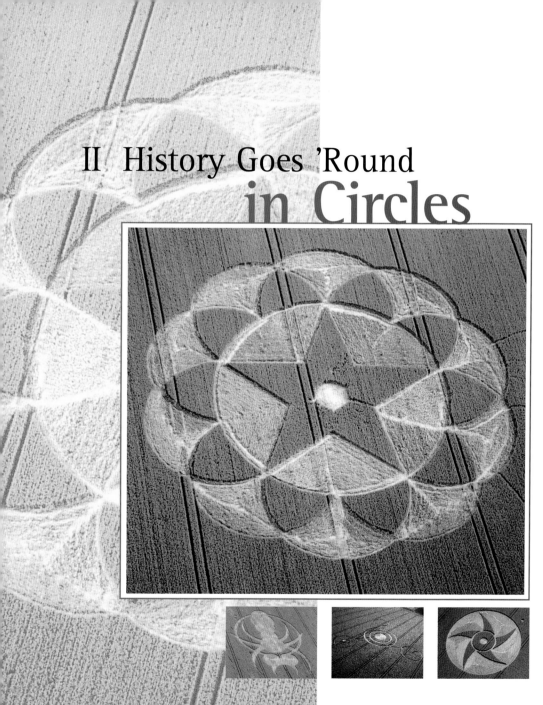

First Circles in the Fields

It was at the beginning of the 1980s that crop circles first attracted public attention. On August 15, 1980, the *Wiltshire Times* published a report about three strange circular symbols that had appeared in the oat fields near Westbury, Wilshire County, South England. Each of the circles had a diameter of 22 yards (20 m). Nothing like that had ever been seen before. No one could find an explanation for it.[1]

A year later, Patrick Delgado, a retired British electrical engineer, came across three circles in a grain field near the city of Winchester in Wiltshire. They lay in the valley of Cheesefoot Head east of Winchester, not far from expressway A272. A large middle circle was flanked by two smaller, identical circles on the axis. Pat Delgado was so impressed that he informed the media.

A widespread theory for explaining the puzzling circles at the time was that they might have been landing places for unidentified flying objects (UFOs). However, over the course of the years this idea has proven unreasonable because of the increasing complexity and number of crop circle formations.

Two years later, in 1983, crop circles turned up again in the valley of Cheesefoot Head—this time five of them. Colin Andrews, an electrical engineer at a British power plant, stopped his car at the edge of the road along "Devil's Punch Bowl," as the valley is commonly known by locals. He'd noticed a group of people gathered near Telegraph Hill, which towers above Winchester at the height of 551 feet (167 m). As he looked into the valley he saw a "gigantic formation of five circles, a large one in the middle and four small ones around it." As Michael Hesemann writes in his book, *Crop Circles*: "Andrews was overpowered by what he saw: the sheer symmetry of the pattern, the position of the wheat plants, which seemed to form large spirals, all of that was so unbelievable and so fascinating that it immediately attracted him with its magic. He climbed down the slope to look at the formation close up. He considered various possibilities as to how someone could have created this symbol but rejected them in the same moment. All of what he saw here appeared to this bone-dry engineer, who considered himself grounded in reality, to be the challenge of his life.... He was the first to make a path through the dry, shining brown grain to take preliminary measurements. The large circle was 17.5 yards (16 m) wide; the diameter of the four satellite circles was 4.5 yards (4 m) each."[2] Colin Andrews has not given up yet on his search for the meaning of the crop circle puzzle.

In the same year, Andrews met Pat Delgado. Together the two engineers wanted to document further examples of crop circles,

III. 13

observations, and eyewitness accounts, and they struck it rich. They found a report of a single circle discovered in 1975 in a wheat field at a farm near Winchester. Following that one there was a second circle the next year (III. 13). The first group formation, consisting of five circles, turned up in 1978 only a few miles from Winchester in the hamlet of Headbourne. In 1981 two additional circles had been found in southern England at "Devil's Punch Bowl," where Pat Delgado had observed the three-part formation. In 1982 four individual circles were discovered—and in 1983, six more individual circles. In addi-

tion, in the same year, three formations turned up, each consisting of five circles arranged together. As with the formation at Winchester, which Colin Andrews had measured, each had a large circle in the center and four circles like little satellites around it, an arrangment much like the number five on a die in a set of dice.

A year later a similar five-part formation attracted special attention: it was discovered by Denis Healey on July 27, 1984, at Alfriston in the county of East Sussex. The well-known English politician was an amateur photographer and took several photos of

III. 13: Single circle at Silbury Hill. The phenomenon began with simple circles.

III. 14: "The Mowing Devil," drawing from 1678

III. 15: Diagram from the 1980s (from *The Crop Circle Enigma* by Ralph Noyes)

Ill. 14

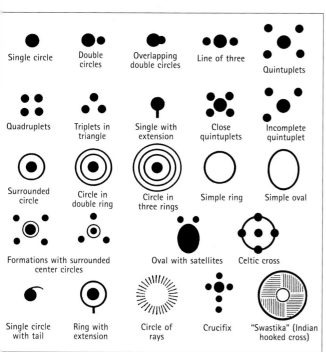

Single circle	Double circles	Overlapping double circles	Line of three	Quintuplets
Quadruplets	Triplets in triangle	Single with extension	Close quintuplets	Incomplete quintuplet
Surrounded circle	Circle in double ring	Circle in three rings	Simple ring	Simple oval
Formations with surrounded center circles		Oval with satellites	Celtic cross	
Single circle with tail	Ring with extension	Circle of rays	Crucifix	"Swastika" (Indian hooked cross)

Ill. 15

symmetrical crop circle constellations found not far from his home. "As the news trickled out that this prominent man (today Lord Healey) had photographed something very unusual outside the front door of his house, it didn't take long until his pictures found their way to the Rainbow Press," writes Andy Thomas in his book, *Vital Signs*. For the first time the subject of crop circles in England reached a wide audience and was the talk of the town. "Questions about the origin of these formations suddenly became the subject of conversation, and soon the broader media took up the subject. Unintentionally through his photographs, Lord Healey had brought greater publicity to crop circles in England."[3]

According to Michael Hesemann, the first "documented" case of a crop circle in England goes back to 1972. Historians and anthropologists even suppose that August 15, 1972, could have been the "hour of birth" of the phenomenon—observed by two eyewitnesses. "The grain flattened like a lady's fan opening up. A perfect circle resulted in less than a minute, while a very high-pitched tone could be heard." This is the way in which a British man, Arthur Shuttlewood, experienced the origin of a crop circle at Star Hill on the outskirts of his home town, the southern English town of Warminster.[4]

Shuttlewood's companion, the American radio journalist Bryce Bond, described the event as follows: "Suddenly I heard a sound. It was as though something was pressing the wheat down. There was no wind during this night. I looked around. The moon had just come out, was shining brightly, and here before my eyes a large imprint was formed. The wheat was pressed down in a counter-clockwise formation. 'It' somehow had the shape of a triangle and was about 8 yards (7 m) across. I stood there for several minutes and felt goose bumps over my entire body, noticed a sweet smell and was surrounded by warm air." Bryce Bond went on: "As we were still discussing it, Arthur discovered more imprints: a circle 11 yards (10 m) in diameter (Ill. 13) and another, cigar-shaped, imprint. The wheat was always shaped into a clockwise spiral form."[5]

On the other hand, it is a "widespread common assumption" that crop circles are phenomena of recent times, maintains Lucy Pringle, who has photographed these grain-field formations from the air and has collected eyewitness accounts since the beginning of the 1990s. She quotes an elderly inhabitant of the southern English county of Sussex who can remember "absolutely clearly" having played in crop circles as a small child: "In two particular fields they turned up regularly over the course of three or four years. Two, sometimes three circles were in the field, swirled flat and with clearly defined borders. A winding path only a half inch narrower connected the circles.... The grown-ups took no notice of them. No one would have dreamed of taking photos of them because of the huge amount of work they had to do, or to turn to the media, let alone to create them themselves! Because they meant a loss of harvest, and bread was scarce during the wartime." Moona Beswick, from Hare in Hertfordshire County, reports similar memories, as can numerous older inhabitants of Wiltshire County.

For that reason one 84-year-old native of Pewsey wondered why in the 1990s there was "sudden excitement and great interest in the circles," which he had "grown up with."[6]

Several researchers see the "Mowing Devil" (Ill. 14) as much older evidence of the crop circle phenomenon. The drawing from 1678 shows the devil in an oval circle cutting wheat with his scythe. The place of origin of the picture and exact date of the event portrayed cannot be determined. It illustrates the legend of a farmer who refused to pay the money demanded by a field worker. "Let the devil mow it!" he said with a curse. "And so it happened," the legend goes, "that in that very night the oat field glowed as though it was standing in flames. But the next morning it had been mowed so perfectly by the devil or by a lower spirit that no mortal could have possibly done it."[7]

Almost 300 depictions of crop circles appear in Terry Wilson's 1980 book *The Secret History of Crop Circles*. Twenty-five of the formations have exact times and places given from the era before World War II. There is even a photograph of a circle formation that lay near Bow Hill, not far from Chichester in West Sussex County, according to author Andy Thomas. There are military aerial photographs from 1943 of a crop circle formation near Tangmere in West Sussex County, also not far from Chichester. Although the Royal Air Force carried out many flights during World War II over all of

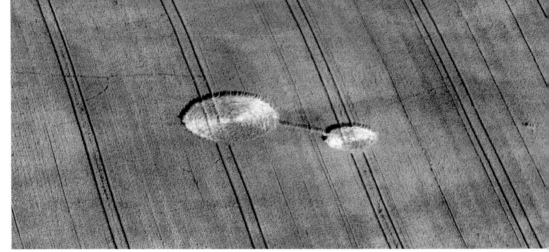

Ill. 16

south England, there are no other RAF aerial photos known that show anything similar.[8]

Michael Hesemann mentions rumors of two circles from 1946 on Pepperbox Hill near Salisbury. In 1955 there was supposedly a crop circle, between Epson and Mickleham in Surrey County, that was inspected by three curious people who agreed in their reports of a "rainbow-colored appearance of light, which floated several yards above the field."[9]

"There were also crop circles even earlier," Andy Thomas writes in his book, *Vital Signs*, "but they were much less common than nowadays. In the course of the years their number suddenly increased and a real jump in their development took place."[10]

1985–1989: Figures Grow out of Circles

In 1985 amateur flyer Busty Taylor joined Colin Andrews and Patrick Delgado. For the first time they were able to view new aerial

Ill. 17

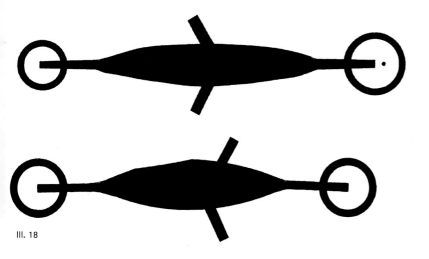

III. 18

photos, taken by the pilot, of crop circle formations. On August 4, 1985, Taylor took photos from the air of five crop circles in the well-known die-like arrangement, with a larger central circle and four outer circles, near Clatford. Taylor was a great catch for the research duo: he could comb the countryside with his plane. The team was no longer dependent on press reports and chance phone calls from farmers and people who had discovered circles.[11]

Taylor, Andrews, and Delgado discovered a good dozen circles in 1986. In 1987 there were suddenly—when counted separately—almost 40 circles in grain fields of Wiltshire and Hampshire Counties: circles, rings, concentric circles, formations of three and of five. Another step in the direction of more complex formations developed on August 8, 1987, when a circle 33 yards (30 m) across with a double ring was discovered in Bratton near Warminster.[12]

The following year, 1988, was distinguished by a further evolution. Ralph Noyes mentions in his book, *The Circles in the Grain*, a "circle with a double ring on the outside" in the "Punch Bowl" near Winchester, an area already known for these. "Then three single circles in a triangular formation appeared as well, in spite of the increased watchfulness of the farmers." The area near Silbury Hill became the center of attention in this summer too, where every year since then numerous crop circle figures have appeared: "On the morning of July 15, 1988 a circle with a five-part configuration appeared in a field south of Silbury Hill, easily visible from the very busy Highway A4; on July 26 a second one appeared, which was directly next to the first at an angle of approximately 45 degrees. About a week later three additional single circles appeared."[13] Michael Hesemann adds that one of these new circles—there were now a

total of 13—lay so perfectly that if you extended the formation lengthwise the two five-fold configurations could be one part of a cross.[14]

"Up to the end of August there were six 'five-fold formations,' mostly in the region around Silbury Hill. Then once again the phenomenon developed further. On September 10 Colin Andrews found a formation that for him was the most fascinating to date: a 'quintuplet' whose satellite circles were joined together by a ring right next to a 'double ringer' near Charity Downs.... The stalks in the ring were woven in and out of one another in a complicated way." Altogether about 120 crop circles appeared, many more even than the previous year, as Hesemann summarized.[15]

In 1989 the number of crop circles exploded to 305. Likewise, interest in the circles grew by great leaps and bounds. In the spring of 1989 Colin Andrews and Pat Delgado went public with their book, *Circular Evidence*. In a very short period of time it landed in tenth place on the British bestseller list. The German translation, *Kreisrunde Zeichen*, sold 85,000 copies a year later. When even the English queen put *Circular Evidence* on her summer reading list, the book was guaranteed a place in the mass media.

Crop circles appeared now in all of England and even in Scotland. And around Silbury Hill in southern England 40 circles had been discovered by the end of the season, in contrast to 15 the previous year. "And their shapes became more and more complicated. The 'Quintuplet' of the previous year now

III. 19

grew with the addition of a sixth circle, which transformed them into long-armed crosses. A circle with a bent tail appeared near Cheesefoot Head. This double-ringed type turned up more frequently, and a circle near Beckhampton, not far from Silbury Hill, had the considerable diameter of 39 yards (35 m)." On August 12, 1989, "the most perfect crop circle the world had ever seen" appeared on the land of farmer Mike Bucknell near Winterbourne Stoke in the vicinity of Amesbury in Wiltshire. The circle, which was about 20 yards (18.5 m) in diameter, was notable because of its cross shape—with combed stalks pointing in all four directions—enclosed by a bordering ring one yard wide. A preview of the 1990s?[16] (Ill. 15)

1990: Quantum Leap

The circle year began early. Already in April a group of small ringed circles and also several large circles up to 60 yards (55 m) in diameter showed up in Wiltshire. At the beginning of May two large three-ringed formations, a type that had its premier in 1989, surrounded by four satellites in the middle ring, appeared simultaneously. The precise rings were mostly only 6 to 9 inches (15 to 22 cm) wide and a phenomenon in themselves. Striking for 1990 was the fact that, according to Hesemann, "subsequent improvements" were made to various crop circle designs.

For 10 days in June a "night watch," or nightly observation of the area, was organized by locals in the vicinity of Silbury Hill. The members of the surveillance groups claim to have heard strange noises during this time. In addition, George Wingfield, one of the organizers, claims to have seen "mysterious lights which moved slowly and rather low above the stalks of the wheat field." A similar occurrence is said to have taken place afterwards at a circle at Milk Hill near Alton Barnes. And, Wingfield explained, in every field where he and his companions had observed appearances of lights, "grapeshots"—very small, often circular or spiral shapes in the grain, usually no larger than half a yard (0.5 m)—were discovered afterwards.[17] Grapeshots often lie near larger formations but also appear individually or in small groups in the field.

But 1990 brought even more surprises: crop circles appeared in the form of "pictograms" in undreamed-of variety. The first

III. 20

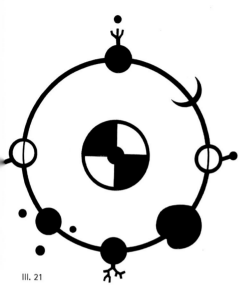

Ill. 19: The legendary "Triangle" of Barbury Castle, July 17, 1991 (Photo Richard Wintle)

Ill. 20: "Mandelbrot Set," beginning of the fractal geometric figures, Ickleton, August 12, 1991 (Diagram Wolfgang Schindler)

Ill. 21: "The Dharma Wheel" at Silbury Hill, August 17, 1992 (Diagram Wolfgang Schindler)

Ill. 22: "Star of Bythorn," September 4, 1993 (Diagram Wolfgang Schindler)

was found May 23rd at Cheesefoot Head. The second and the third appeared in the same area on June 2nd and 15th. A week later the fourth symbol was discovered at Lichfield. All these figures had in common an "axis" connected by circles, making them resemble dumbbells (Ill. 16). Additional elements, such as rings, concentric arches, or short parallel lines, were present also. Often the axis lay parallel to or on top of the tramlines in the field; sometimes it was in a completely different direction. The pictograms were getting longer and more impressive. On June 28th, a dumbbell 55 yards (50 m) long turned up at Longwood Estate. A week later an 81-yard (74 m) pictogram was found at Crawley Downs.[18]

Then, barely a week later, on July 11, 1990, the sensation of the year arrived: in the valley of Pewsey near Alton Barnes a 185-yard-long (168 m) figure was discovered. Pat Delgado describes his first reaction: "Soon we saw the strangest pictogram we had ever seen in the field below us. The pattern is so complicated that an exact description would fill several pages....The circles were exactly and clearly formed and the center consisted of classic narrow spiral twists with sharply defined borders. On the middle path the grain was upright. As usual it was untouched. Especially the key-shaped forms caught our attention because of their composition of squares and rectangles. This combination characterized the configuration of the entire formation. The difference from the pictograms of former weeks, which were already very complex, was breathtaking and the increase in variety of symbols just fan-

tastic." Only a few miles to the west, at Stanton St. Bernard, a similar pictogram approximately 165 yards (150 m) long appeared (Ill. 17).

Photos of the pictograms in the valley of Pewsey were published all over the world. Soon, floods of curiosity seekers stormed the fields at Alton Barnes. The pictogram was heavily damaged by the thousands of visitors who trampled over the grain.[19]

Even greater surprises followed. In August, at Hazeley Farm Fields and near Allington Down, pictograms were discovered second not even to those at Alton Barnes in size, complexity, and precision. Two of the additional figures lay on Pepperbox Hill. And on August 5th, a spiral-shaped figure resembling a rolled-up snake, which opened up at the end into a wound-up question mark, appeared near Westbury "before the lenses of two night-viewer cameras."[20]

1991: The Entire World Watches Southern England

Crop circles reached their temporary culmination in number, size, and complexity in 1991. In the middle of April a circle was discovered only a mile or so from Tor Hill at Glastonbury. The next couple of months were quiet. But then there was hardly a day without a new discovery. Sixty pictograms of greater or lesser complexity were recorded by Jürgen Krönig in southern England.[21] Over 400 individual symbols were counted among them, according to the crop circle researcher and author.[22] This statement demonstrates why, from at least 1990 onward, it made more sense to count whole pictograms, formations, figures—or whatever you wish to call them—instead of individual circles or elements.

Among the 1991 formations were numerous dumbbell and key-shaped pictograms similar to those of the previous year. Several of the 1991 figures were practically identical.

In addition to those came the "insect-o-grams" and "dolphin-o-grams" (Ill. 18); that is, pictograms that remind you of insects or dolphins. The "insect-o-grams," which actually looked more like snails, added a new dimension to the phenomenon, in Hesemann's opinion: "While there had been more 'classic' symbols appearing in the grain fields up to now, they now had an almost comical, bizarre effect and seemed to have no meaning at first glance."[23] From the end of July to the end of August seven "dolphin-o-grams" were discovered, elongated, spindle-shaped, often with "flippers," and always closed off at the ends with a circle.

The real surprise of the season came in the middle of July: "In the night between the 17th and 18th of July, in a barley field in the vicinity of prehistoric Hillfort's Barbury Castle, a configuration was created which put everything previously seen in its shadow," writes Jürgen Krönig. "This involves an unusually exquisite pictogram, a combination of triangle, circles, rings, arches and straight lines."[24] (Ill. 19)

But four weeks later, at the very end of the 1991 "circle season," a symbol drew even more attention: On August 12th the depiction of a "Mandelbrot Set" (a geometric figure named

for its discoverer, the French mathematician Benoit Mandelbrot) appeared in a field near Ickleton, Cambridgeshire (Ill. 20). Krönig states: "This involves a mathematical figure of fractal geometry, which could only be created with the help of computers. It can be interpreted as a symbol for the chaotic transition from a mathematical order to the next highest order."[25] The press interpreted this as a prank carried out by mathematics students from Cambridge University, where Mandelbrot was teaching. But even the British sci-

III. 23

III. 23: "Two Moons," Furze Knoll, May 7, 1994, rape

III. 24: "The Spider," Barbury Castle, July 7, 1994, 57 yards (52 m)

III. 25: "The Scorpion of Devizes," July 14, 1994, 187 yards (170 m)

III. 24

ence magazine *New Scientist* conceded that it would not be possible to draw a Mandelbrot figure without a computer, let alone put one in a wheat field.[26]

The formations at Barbury Castle and Ickleton would be "the only obvious figures which could be analyzed mathematically," according to Jürgen Krönig. "Whether the other formations in the southern English wheat fields also contain mathematical contexts is difficult to say." At least in part they do, he supposes.

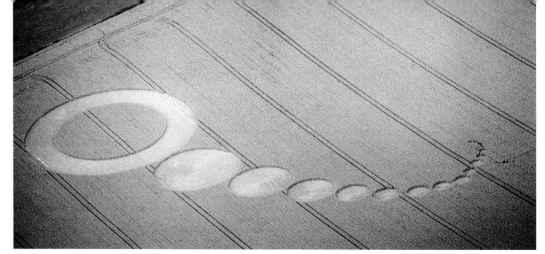

III. 26

1992-1993: Years of Disappointment

The 1992 season didn't fulfill the high expectations awakened by the two previous years. The weather was one reason. After four dry summers, which made searching for crop circles enchanting excursions into the countryside, many fields in 1992 were so disheveled by storms that they were no longer possible "canvases" for figures. Also, many farmers were less cooperative than they had been. They began to demand money for access to their fields. And because of the warm, humid summer, they brought in their harvests early. Hesemann says: "Visitors were greeted by stubble instead of waving grain fields. The consternation this caused was not lessened by the reports that they heard. The dramatic evolution of the phenomenon seemed over. The total number of circles and pictograms was less than the two previous years."[27]

Nonetheless, even in 1992, Michael Hesemann claims to have discovered "about 30

circles and pictograms" in South England (III. 21). Among them were two "gigantic snails," one of which was in the valley of Alton Barnes, the other near Pewsey. "A symbol for the slowing down of the energy and the snail's pace at which the consciousness of humankind comes to terms with this?" Hesemann broods in his writing.[28]

The year 1993 was a low point for "croppies"—and not just because so few crop circle formations had appeared since 1992 compared to 1990 and 1991. The media, too, lost most of their interest in the circle phenomenon. Over the past year various individuals and groups had been successful at convincing the press and television that all the geometric configurations in the fields of southern England were "handmade." Suddenly the paranormal phenomenon seemed to have been "unmasked as a hoax" (see pages 101-4) and the subject was dead as far as the media were concerned.

In spite of that some impressive figures appeared in 1993. The concentration of dis-

III. 27

III. 28

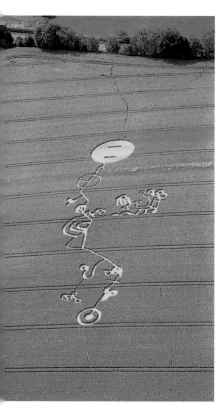

III. 26: "The Scorpion of Wilsford," July 16, 1994

III. 27: "The Eye of Horus," East Field, July 21, 1994

III. 28: "Galaxy" mowed down at West Kennet, July 24, 1994 (compare III. 11)

III. 29: "The Labyrinth," West Kennet, July 24, 1994, 132 yards (120 m)

Cambridgeshire. A pentagon encircled a pentagram (five-sided star), and in the figure's center were a circle and three concentric rings. Surrounding this were ten "blossom leaves," which in turn were enclosed in a still larger circle (III. 22). This last formation of the year—it turned up on September 4, 1993, in an overly ripe wheat field that was harvested shortly afterwards—fired up new emotions and discussion about the origin of crop circles.[31]

1994: Crop Circles Are Back

After the lean years of 1992 and 1993, crop circles returned to the fields in great numbers and in a way that created great excitement. What luck for all those people who had only begun to investigate this phenomenon in southern England in 1994. For several of us our first forays into the grain fields were the beginning of a long journey that has continued with no end in sight.

On May 7th a crop circle with two equally large crescent moons, which complemented each other like positive and negative sides, appeared in a rape field at Furze Knoll, Wiltshire (III. 23). At Barbury Castle a 57-yard-long (52 m) bee- or spider-like animal symbol was discovered on July 7th. Seldom before had there been a symbol commanding so much awe (III. 24). A second animal symbol turned up a week later at Bishops Cannings: complete with "eyes" and "pincers," this formation became known as "The Scorpion of Devizes" in crop circle history (III. 25). At 187 yards (170 m) long, it was to become the largest of this new type,

coveries moved for a time to West Sussex County in July, where two five-part formations—each with a large central circle and four smaller satellites connected by a ring—appeared at a place called Somting. A 66-yard-long (60 m) cross-shaped formation, which was discovered on July 7th near Charley Knoll in the vicinity of Loughborough, stirred up even greater interest.

Also unusual was a large ring found four days later in East Kennet, Wiltshire. It extended over three different fields and had as its center the crossing of two country highways. Two weeks later, a good hundred yards away, a second figure appeared in one of the fields. Another two formations were discovered in the "classic" surroundings of Alton Barnes at Cherhill. One was a key-shaped pictogram over 110 yards (100 m) long.[29]

Hesemann claims to have counted about 25 circles and pictograms in the middle of August during three flights over Wiltshire County.[30] A big, very late surprise of the season was a completely concentric pattern found near the little village of Bythorn in

the "animal series," which essentially characterized the year's formations.

The farmer in whose field "The Scorpion" was found reacted very indignantly—as he has since, whenever new formations turn up in his fields (see also page 60). On July 16th—the same day 21 comet fragments collided with the planet Jupiter—a configuration a good hundred yards long, also similar to a scorpion, emerged near Wilsford. Twenty-one circles diminishing in size and resembling a tail (or perhaps 21 fragments of comets?) trailed a large ring 44 yards (40 m) in diameter (Ill. 26). Also, near Cholsey in Oxfordshire County, a new gigantic scorpion 176 yards (160 m) long appeared, showing its pincers. Was this third scorpion pictogram part of a "huge effort of a team of forgers, who would need two hours even to get from one place to the other by car, or actually the 'real phenomenon'?" Michael Hesemann asked himself.[32]

On July 21st a 88-yard (80 m) circle resembling an eye appeared in East Field at Alton Barnes, a location that by now had become legendary (Ill. 27). While a research group led by Colin Andrews examined the freshly made symbol in the field, an unusual incident occurred: A military helicopter flew very low over the field as though it wanted to investigate something. Suddenly the research team noticed a small, blinking light in the grain. As the strange object moved swiftly, like a bolt of lightning, across the field to the other side of the valley, the pilot temporarily lost his orientation, then continued his investigation. This event was captured on video.[33] A wide variety of

eyewitnesses independently reported the appearances of small, round objects of light. The question of whether they were directly related to the crop circles still has not been answered. We can only confirm that similar appearances of light also were observed at night at Milk Hill in the vicinity of East Field and that they too were investigated by helicopter.

On July 1st, opposite "Stone Avenue" between Avebury and West Kennet, the first of three "galaxy-type" formations appeared. But their existence was only of short duration, according to Andy Thomas.[34] The field's farmer mowed down all the little circular figures and the points of the "crescent moon" before the day was out (Ills. 11 and 28). A practically identical crop circle came into being three weeks later on July 23rd near West Stowell in the vicinity of Pewsey (see pages 19-20). It had a diameter of almost 66 yards (60 m).

On the morning of July 24th alone, six new figures were discovered in the fields of Wiltshire. One of them, between Avebury and West Kennet, was a labyrinth that spread out over 132 yards (120 m). It included several winding dead-end "streets" and finally ended in a large circle (Ill. 29). A really gigantic key-shaped pictogram turned up on July 26th during this particularly active period of time, at Ashbury in Oxfordshire County. The figure's 832-yard (756 m) length broke all size records by far (Ills. 30, 62). Also, the night before July 27th—in which, according to Hesemann, six new formations had already appeared[35]—an elegant three-moon crop circle 121 yards (110 m) in

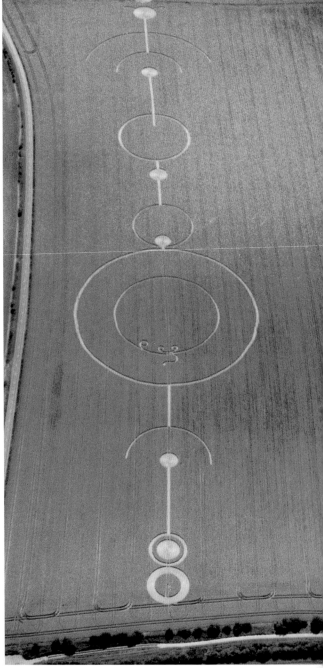

III. 30

III. 30: "The Langpi Pictogram of Ashbury," July 26, 1994, 832 yards (756 m)

III. 31: "The Triple Moon," Oliver's Castle, July 27, 1994, 121 yards (110 m), wheat (see also III. 206)

III. 32: Infinity symbol, West Overton, July 28, 1994

III. 31

III. 32

At Hackpen Hill, where crop circles have been sighted again and again, one figure consisting of 10 circles turned up (III. 33). It was about 154 yards (140 m) long and ended in three "grapeshots." And a 94-yard-wide (85 m) crop circle resembling a Gothic symbol appeared on August 5th in the vicinity of Hungerford. Its geometric form resembled the well-known "creation symbol," which had also appeared in several previous crop circles (IIIs. 34, 63, 199, 200).

In the middle of August 1994, the season of surprises reached its culmination: On August 10th, on the north side of the earthen wall at Avebury, a figure 110 yards (100 m) in diameter emerged from the morning twilight; it would overshadow everything seen up until then (III. 35). Strangely, on the following morning, August 11th, it had been enlarged by several elements, unnoticed—in spite of a "night watch" from atop the earthen wall. In other words, it arose in two stages, unlike other formations. The "Spider Web," with 10 spokes, also called "Dream Catcher" and of absolutely breathtaking beauty, presented itself from a bird's-eye view like a golden flower in the shining late summer days, harmoniously completing the ancient ring wall site of Avebury.

Additional crop circles discovered later that season paled in comparison to the "Dream Catcher." In the middle of August a figure around 50 yards (45 m) in diameter also appeared near Avebury: 13 circles in descending order of size and an adjoining crescent moon, the entirety forming a circle (III. 36). A simple 57-yard (52 m) crop circle

diameter was discovered in a wheat field beneath the popular viewing area at Oliver's Castle, creating a stir (IIIs. 31, 206). It was a convincing example that simplicity and harmony are by no means incompatible.

The widely recognized mathematic sign for infinity, a flattened figure eight, appeared on July 28th at West Overton (IIIs. 32, 196). The crop circle was clearly visible from Highway A4 between Marlborough and Avebury. It was the first of more than 200 crop circles that this book's authors have seen and studied over the years. Right after entering the formation, a few of us noticed goose bumps on our skin. At the time this reaction was strange and puzzling to us. Since then, however, we and other crop circle researchers have become used to such experiences.

with seven rings appeared on August 24th at Froxfield (Ill. 37). Did it represent a constellation of stars? And for that reason was it an advance announcement of the 1995 crop circles, which often resembled astronomical pictures?

1995: "Planets" and "Asteroids"

The year 1995 was unusual for southern England in terms of climate. The summer was long, often almost unbearably hot and dry. This made fieldwork for crop circle researchers difficult. The midday siesta, which in southern nations is used to bridge the hottest midday hours by resting in the shade, was gladly adopted temporarily in England as an everyday event. The year also was notable for two other reasons: the emergence of formation motifs that often resembled planetary systems and a widespread public attention on "fakes." At a time when crop circles announced themselves again in great number and impressive variety after two weak years, the concept of "forgeries" reentered the spotlight (see pages 101-4). Too many individuals and groups blabbed about supposed crop circle "secrets" to the media, often without any authentic proof. This caused many people to become indifferent to appearances before the new ones in the fields could reawaken their interest. Even quite a number of former researchers and other once-interested people had dismissed crop-circle phenomena summarily. The skepticism, however, did not seem to bother the crop circles. On the contrary.

On May 29th, along Highway A4 between Beckhampton and Cherhill, a crop circle 70 yards (64 m) in diameter appeared among the low barley plants (Ill. 38). In it there was a spiral-shaped path, laid out very precisely over the considerable distance of 495 yards (450 m), which led from the outer ring to the inner circle. On June 1st, a wheel with four spiral spokes, the "Catherine's Wheel," appeared in Alfreston in Sussex County (Ill. 39). Measuring 94 yards (85 m) in diameter it was the largest symbol that had appeared

Ill. 33

Ill. 34

III. 35

in this county up till then and was easily
visible from the highway.

A circular formation of "quintuplets," with
four satellite circles then forming again by
"quintuplets," was discovered June 12th on
Telegraph Hill near Cheesefoot Head on the
A272 southwest of Winchester (III. 40). The
figure, though a much simpler example,
appeared to be another of many fractal
structures, which appeared in great number a
year after the "Mandelbrot Diagram" of 1991.

Fractal geometric figures were distinguished by their "satellites," which were
copies of the main structure. The formation
at Telegraph Hill was a fractal figure with
one repetition. Many say that this symbol
has a connection to the planet Jupiter,
which we know to be encircled by the four
main moons discovered by Galileo: Io,
Europa, Ganymede, and Callisto.

On June 19th at Cow Down, south of
Andover, a crop circle appeared consisting of
three concentric rings. It had a diameter of
94 yards (85 m) and was interspersed with a
zigzag path of seven loops meandering from
the outside to the inside (III. 41). A short distance outside of it were three small circles,
"grapeshots." Six days after its discovery a
strong magnetic abnormality was confirmed:
compass needles strayed far from north.

Amateur pilot John Gibbs, who flew over
crop circles in southern England regularly
until 1998, observed, as did other flyers, that
such compass deviations were not unusual
when flying above the figures.

Then, on June 19th, the most complex
pictogram of the year was discovered in a
wheat field near Bishops Sutton: a
schematic representation of the solar system, apparently, with a distinct "asteroid
belt" (III. 42). Three rings and 96 circles
formed a diameter of 149 yards (135 m).
("Asteroid belt" refers to debris of various
sizes that orbits the central heavenly body
on a determined path. This, of course, is the
case in our solar system, with the main belt
occupying a path between Mars and
Jupiter—a "fifth planetary orbit" occupied
not by a planet, but by fragments.) Another
unbelievably precise crop circle with the
characteristics of the solar system, this one
97 yards (88 m) in diameter, emerged at the
end of June southeast of Winchester (III. 44).
Four "orbits" around a central circle were
visible. In our solar system these correspond
to the planets Mercury, Venus, Earth, and
Mars, proceeding outward from the sun. The
formation's "fifth orbit," which lies outside
and is represented by 65 circles, again
resembled the asteroid belt. It is striking in
this configuration that in the "third orbit,"
which in our solar system would represent
the earth, the "planet" is missing. An earlier
"solar system" 88 yards (80 m) in size was
also sighted at the beginning of the month
near Bratton Castle, one of the Iron Age hill-
side fortresses in the vicinity of Warminster.

The middle of July was a particularly active time during the 1995 season. South of Andover an arrangement of 16 rings 149 yards (135 m) in diameter emerged in a grain field (Ill. 43). Unusual for this crop circle were the many—44 altogether—grapeshot circlets of various small sizes. Many of them lay "unreachable" between the tractor paths, without the slightest indication of footpaths leading to them through the grain. A crop circle resembling the earth's magnetic field, which surrounds our planet in many belts, also was discovered in mid-July in the vicinity of East Meon, southeast of Winchester (Ill. 45). At the same time came word of a second crop circle in the vicinity of East Meon. The 62-yard-wide (56 m) formation combined crescent moons of various sizes in a most precise manner (Ill. 46).

A crop circle 55 yards (50 m) in diameter, which appeared in the middle of July at Winterbourne Basset, north of Avebury, showed a well-known geometric representation, a "vector equilibrium" (Ill. 47). In this figure, which is based on the work of Pythagoras, a circle, triangle, and square are combined in such a way that a three-dimensional figure results. Likewise, in the middle of July near Kingsclere, southeast of Newbury, "The Fire Wheel," also called "Shiriken," was discovered at the foot of Watership Down Hills (Ill. 48). This figure, reminiscent of a rotating pentagram, lay in the farmland of the musical composer Andrew Lloyd Weber. Since then, the historian and UFO specialist Michael Hesemann has been hoping that the creator of such famous musicals as "Cats" and "Phantom of the Opera" would

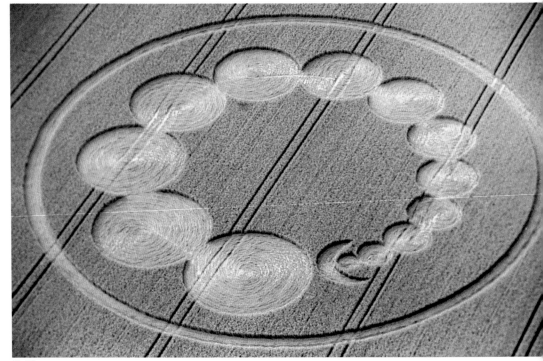

Ill. 36

be inspired by the crop circle to write a new composition entitled "Phantom in the Cornfield."[36]

Around July 16, an especially beautiful circle 88 yards (80 m) in diameter emerged south of Newbury. The labyrinth-like design lay on a slope directly facing Highway A303 and could be viewed easily from passing vehicles (Ill. 49). On July 20th, a new type of crop circle only 24 yards (22 m) across was discovered east of Andover (Ill. 50). What is striking about this is the information given by two older local people who claimed to have observed the appearance of lights in

the sky at the same place eight years earlier: a "thin ring with eight position lights" appeared, which to them echoed abstractly the shape of the crop circle.

Around July 25, two shapeless and, when viewed from the air, not terribly impressive circles appeared out of nowhere under a high power line at Roundway Hill near Devizes (Ill. 51). Toward six in the evening three of us entered this field. To our surprise the two circles lay in narrow layers of grain forming an S-shape, leading from the center to the outside into the field (Ill. 52). This created an outer fringe at the standing border,

Ill. 36: "13-moon Cycle" near Avebury, middle of August 1994, 50 yards (45 m)

Ill. 37: "Pleiades," Fraxfield, August 24, 1994, 57 yards (52 m)

Ill. 38: "The Spirals," Beckhampton, May 29, 1995, 70 yards (64 m), barley

III. 37

diameter? Had it read our thoughts? Or is this just one of the "coincidences" that accompanied us so frequently on our quest for crop circles? Are we humans perhaps also involved in the process of circle creation through our thoughts? The surprising formation—just a ring and two circles—reminded us again that beauty is also found in simplicity (III. 53).

1996: Year of the Fractals

For a long while quiet reigned in the main crop circle regions in the south of England, around Wiltshire and Hampshire Counties. The end of May approached. Our third crop circle summer stood before us. Not a single report worth mentioning had come as yet from Britain. A few circles had turned up, though—for example, two near Girten on May 14th in Cambridgeshire (III. 54). But figures of this sort no longer awakened our urge for research. Our patience was tried—until shortly after the middle of June, when a promising report came from Ulrich Kox, an industrious German crop circle photographer for many years: on the morning of June 17th, a huge crop circle formation 242 yards (220 m) long was discovered in East Field near Alton Barnes (III. 55). Altogether 89 circles of different sizes portrayed a "double helix," which resembled the genetic thread of life, a DNA sequence. Well, finally! Our long wait was rewarded with a high point right at the beginning of the season. "Oh, it's a beauty! It's a beauty!" These were the only words the American crop circle researcher Peter Sørensen could find as he stepped into

III. 38

which did not allow for any regularly shaped form. We were all exhausted by the heat and the long hours of work, and decided to lie down a while in the interior of the circle. The loud crackling of the high wires above our heads, however, convinced us to return home. While leaving, one of our group of three pointed to a distant field and commented that he would have "placed a crop circle back there." The next morning, farmer Chris Combe called us again. Another crop circle! When we arrived at the same field we couldn't believe our eyes: the new figure lay at the "suggested" place!

We were not the creators of this formation. All of us had gone to bed rather early the evening before and slept till the break of day. Whoever or whatever had created this harmonious crop circle 82 yards (74 m) in

the new formation for the first time.[37] This impressive, beautiful pictogram was a topic of conversation for years to come.

The season was quiet again until July 7th, when, just across from Stonehenge, one of the most important prehistoric sites in Europe, the next great event in crop circle history took place. Along one of the busiest superhighways of Wiltshire, the expressway A303, the "Julia Set" appeared. It was over 330 yards (300 m) long, twisted into a spiral, and consisted of 151 circles (Ill. 56). It was a fractal figure much like those in mathematics textbooks. For four days, the owner of the field, Farmer Sandell, wouldn't permit field investigations by crop circle researchers. He was convinced this was an evil prank played by nocturnal jokers. But the moment he saw the first aerial photos of "his" field symbols, he could only shake his head in bewilderment: "What, that's in my grain?"(Ill. 57). Finally, work in the field could begin. The sign the farmer placed on the highway, "See Europe's best crop circle!" (Ill. 58), and the nearness to Stonehenge were certainly not the only reasons why over 10,000 visitors streamed into Sandell's field in less than three weeks. Many came to investigate.

Although most crop circles appear between midnight and 6 A.M., the "Julia Set" is testimony to daytime appearances. Farmer Sandell claims to have personally inspected the field on that Sunday morning and not noticed anything unusual. A security guard claims he inspected the adjoining field to the south from Stonehenge with binoculars at 5 P.M. of the same day—also without see-

Ill. 39

ing anything unusual. And the third witness, an amateur pilot who did not wish to be named, flew over the field in question at 5:30 P.M., coming directly from the south. As he flew over the field again half an hour later on his return flight, he immediately noticed the spectacular gigantic formation.

On July 12th, the most beautiful crop circle formation found to date in Essex County

appeared at Littlebury Green. The formation, measuring around 77 yards (70 m), was as harmonious as it was complex (Ill. 59). On July 25th, several smaller crop circles turned up at Roundway Hill near Devizes, one of which drew attention because of its strange symbol (Ill. 60). Only a day later, in Oxfordshire County, a classic creation symbol, overlapping circles known as a "Vesica Pisces,"

Ill. 39: "Catherine's Wheel" of Alfreston, June 1, 1995, 94 yards (85 m)

Ill. 40: "Planet Jupiter," Telegraph Hill, June 12, 1995

Ill. 41: "Zigzag Path," south of Andover, June 19, 1995, 94 yards (85 m)

III. 40

(Ills. 63 and 199), was found. The large figure, 60 yards (55 m) in diameter, was captivating because of its simplicity and exactness.

July 26, 1996, is another date engraved in the annals of crop circles. With a length of 1,485 yards (1350 m), the gigantic symbol discovered in Etchilhampton surpassed all previous figures by far (III. 62; see also III. 30). A few yards beside the main figure, a 35-yard (32 m) circle was found, again with an unusual symbol in the interior and a drop-shaped appendix (III. 61). This motif had already been found in a variant form several days earlier on the other side of the valley at Roundway (III. 60). It hardly seemed possible that the most extensive crop circle

formation found until then would be overshadowed completely by another one on the same day. What lay at the farm of the Butler family at Windmill Hill near Avebury, perfect as never before, is and remains one of the most fantastic figures that has ever turned up (Ills. 65, 197). The "Triple Julia Set" measured 286 X 286 yards (260 x 260 m) and covered a surface of over 15 acres (6 ha). With its 194 individual circles, this fractal, an aesthetic wonder, reached a new record in numbers of elements. Stalks of grain were still standing in the center of the circles, which grew smaller and smaller progressing from the inside of the spiral to the outside. The flattened stalks lay around it, alternating in first clockwise then counterclockwise circles.

III. 41

Upon closer examination, the stalks, which were not broken, were completely puzzling. They were bent horizontally at the first growth node, around 4 inches (10 cm) from the ground, as if these nodes had become flexible "knees" for a moment, then immediately turned rigid (Ills. 64, 174). These stalks could not have been flattened by a simple mechanical force (see also pages 101-4).

As though this unbelievable event, which happened in a single night, was not enough for crop circle friends, another highlight came only four days later: on August 2nd a double formation (Ill. 66) appeared at Liddington Castle on the land of Farmer Woodtly. The two figures lay about 110 yards (100 m) apart. One was another fractal figure, and the second represented a slightly oval configuration with two symmetrical axes (Ill. 68).

A week after that the formation known as "The Snowflake" of Oliver's Castle appeared (Ill. 67). This crop circle, with three axes and measuring 110 yards (100 m) in diameter, created a controversy that continues today. An Englishperson claims to have captured on video the actual creation of the crop circle on the day it appeared: two smaller objects of light flitting over the grain in two short sequences each, one after the other, can be seen on the film. During the rounds made by the lights, the stalks of grain were flattened in the field in a matter of a few seconds. As quickly as the "shining balls" had come, they disappeared again. Only the "Snowflake" remained visible.[38]

The year 1996 was special not only because of the number of crop circle symbols that appeared but also because of the figures' size, perfection, and unprecedented complexity and beauty. Again, a "quantum leap."

1997: Stars in the Field

After the unbelievably impressive year of 1996, many people were wondering: would things continue like this? On April 19th, a large "Whirligig" about 61 yards (55 m) across with six crescent moons (Ill. 69) appeared in a rape field at Barbury Castle—

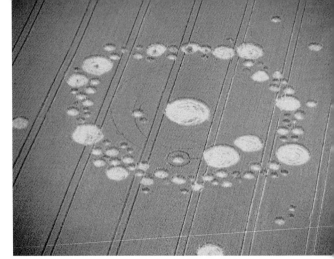

Ill. 42

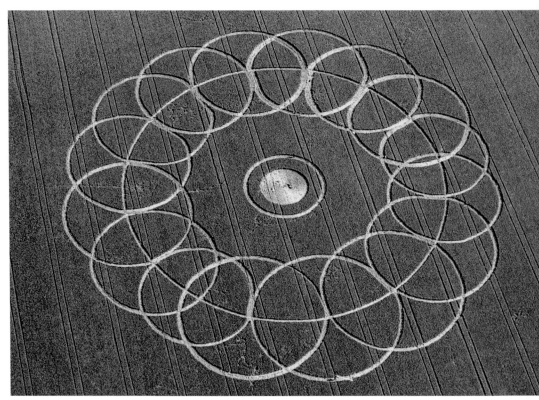

Ill. 43

III. 44

next to the field where the legendary triangle pictogram (see page 28 and III. 19) had
lain. And at the beginning of May, only a little more than a mile (2 km) to the east, the
55-yard-long (50 m) "Tree of Life" appeared.
This sign is a key symbol in the Jewish
cabala (III. 70).

Almost a month of relative quiet passed.
Then, on June 1st at Winterbourne, Bassett,
Wiltshire, the "Harlequin Figure" was discov-

ered (III. 71). This was impressive not so
much for its size or complexity as for the
various arrangements of the barley stalks,
which made the "Harlequin" a refined geometric feast for the eyes.[39]

The approximately 149-yard-wide (135 m)
"Snowflake" at Stonehenge was perhaps two
days old when its appearance was
announced on June 10th (III. 72). Lying in
the same field as 1996's "Julia Set," this fig-

ure with 194 circles had the same number of
elements as the "Triple Julia Set" created at
Avebury. At this point, no one imagined that
this fractal configuration was the beginning
of an impressive series of six-pointed stars.
And the fact that this series invisibly connected important prehistoric sites such as
Hackpen Hill (III. 102), Silbury Hill (Ills. 84,
85), Cley Hill (Ills. 80, 81), Milk Hill (Ills. 94,

41

95, 96), and even Stonehenge may have occurred to only a few people.

On June 15th, at Upsham in Hampshire County, a decorative crop circle only 33 yards (30 m) long appeared (Ill. 73). Several researchers who inspected it were impressed by the circle's interior. A year later this rather modest crop circle again became a subject of discussion, this time as a "shadow formation" in slightly different-colored, standing grain (Ill. 74 of the "Seven-pointed Star of Upham" of 1998; see in this connection page 51). On July 6, 1997, a formation 33 yards (30 m) across with a large central circle, surrounded by 29 small circles forming an outer ring, was reported along Highway A272 southeast of Winchester (Ill. 75). A day later, drivers on Highway M3 at Head-bourne Worthy could observe an easily visible symbol 94 yards (85 m) in diameter in the wheat (Ill. 76). It strongly resembled the "Quinta Essentia," a well-known symbol from religion and philosophy that represents the composition of the earth from the elements of fire, water, air, earth, and ether (Ill. 192).

On July 11th, interest was directed again toward the region around Alton Barnes. In the field opposite the well-known East Field, a large ring formation a good 110 yards (100 m) in size had been discovered in the early morning (Ills. 77, 179). Twelve large, overlapping rings surrounding the central circle in regular intervals lent "Torus," as the crop circle was soon dubbed, a three-dimensional effect when seen from the air. It is important to mention the strange phenomena of light and sound that various people independently observed in the vicinity of the field between 8 P.M. and midnight. "Over a period of several minutes a high humming tone coming at short intervals puzzled me," Jeb Barton, an American tepee maker from Oregon, remembers. He'd noticed the sound at nightfall while walking from Alton Barnes in the direction of West Stowell Farm.[40] Two locals from Alton Priors spoke of "strange rays of light" in the direction of Woodbor-ough Hill, where the new formation was found in the field the next day. And travelers claim to have seen "a sort of bell-shaped light" at Woodborough Hill before midnight. The way in which the stalks in "Torus" were flattened resembles the work of a hair-dresser shaping hair with a hair dryer and

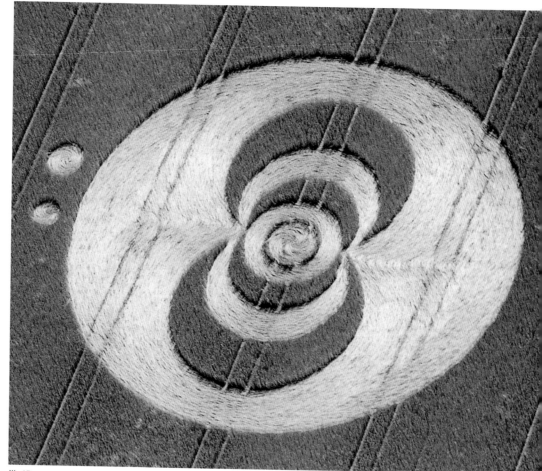

III. 46

III. 45: "Geomagnetic Field," East Meon, mid-July 1995 (Photo Ulrich Kox)

III. 46: "Crescent Moons," East Meon, mid-July 1995, 62 yards (56 m) (Photo Ulrich Kox)

setting gel (III. 78). This style was the mark of several other crop circles in 1997.

An impressive, pentagram-type five-pointed star, a design known among native Americans as a "Hopi Star," left its mark on the countryside around Bishops Cannings near the city of Devizes on July 13th (III. 79; see also III. 194). Measuring 61 yards (55 m) in diameter, it was not especially large but very impressive, with its clearly defined geometry.

Below Cley Hill near Warminster (III. 80), a six-pointed star or, depending on how you view it, a complex hexagon appeared on July 14th (III. 81). Measuring 94 yards (85 m) in diameter, it was clearly smaller than the earlier six-pointed star formation, the "Snowflake" at Stonehenge (III. 72). An animal-shaped figure also appeared again, on July 17th, in Hen Wood, Hampshire (III. 82). It strongly resembled an ant, although it had four body segments instead of three. Inhabitants of the farm near the field told us that two circling helicopters above the wheat field around 3 A.M. had jolted them out of their sleep. The pictogram's interior was dazzling, with wonderfully constructed layers. Inter-

estingly, the flattened surface of the grain was interspersed with thousands of stalks that were still upright (III. 83).

On July 23rd there were again two new crop circles in the fields of Wiltshire. A few hundred yards north of Silbury Hill the morning sun shone on a 99-yard-wide (90 m), extremely complicated fractal star, fresh with dew and surrounded by 126 small circles (III. 84). From a mathematical standpoint this figure resembles a "Koch Snowflake," named for the discoverer Helge von Koch, a pioneer in fractal geometry. Worth noting in this formation as well was the arrangement of the flattened stalks in the interior, which viewed from the air produced a three-dimensional effect (Ill. 85). It has been proven here without any doubt that the complex star could only have come into being the night before July 23rd. That night at dusk, Thomas Peterlunger of Bern, Switzerland, had searched the vicinity with his binoculars for new crop circles without success from atop 132-foot (40 m) high Silbury Hill. Then, toward 11 P.M. from Expressway A4, which runs nearby, two residents of the area saw "strobelike beams of light," which then came down from the sky, penetrating the field in question.

During the same night, a conspicuous crop circle appeared at Oliver's Castle, the same place as 1994's "Triple Moon" (Ills. 31 and 206). The 77-yard (70 m) formation included a distinct initial "S" and two grapeshots (Ill. 86). The center of this crop circle was reminiscent of astrological symbols and had several mystifying details: stalks flattened as if by magic in a clockwise direction (Ill. 87), with growth nodes that were visibly swollen and clearly angled away but not broken (Ill. 174).

A crop circle below Fasbury Forts in Wiltshire must have been several days or weeks old when it was discovered on August 5th (Ill. 92). Its unusual shape merited it the name "Mickey Mouse." Also at the beginning of August, in the vicinity of Liddington Castle, one of England's many prehistoric round earthen wall sites, an entire series of crop circles appeared. The first was a simple circle about 20 yards (18 m) in diameter. Again,

Ill. 47

Farmer Woodtly was the owner of the field. Seized with rage, he rode his tractor around the interior of the circle in curves until the field looked like a motocross track (Ill. 89). A few days later, in spite of Woodtly's increased vigilance, two new circles turned up on his property at the foot of Liddington Castle (Ills. 90, 91). The two circles remained untouched for several days, until early one morning Woodtly was seized with anger. He

got out a combine and mowed the circles, erasing them from the field (Ill. 88; see also Ill. 155).

An especially beautiful double formation, with two circles 55 and 66 yards (50 and 60 m) in diameter, appeared on August 2nd at Etchilhampton in the vicinity of Devizes (Ill. 93), where, during the previous year, a 1,430-yard (1300 m) formation had lain (Ill. 62). You could recognize traces of the earlier

Ill. 47: "Vector Equilibrium," Pythagorean geometry, Winterbourne Bassett, July 23, 1995

Ill. 48: "The Fire Wheel," Watership Down Hill, mid-July 1995

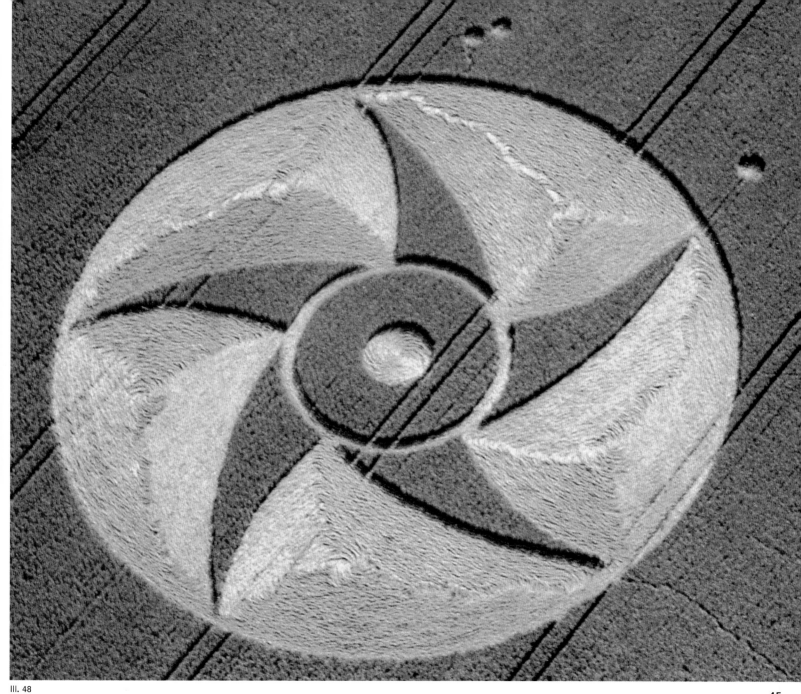

Ill. 49

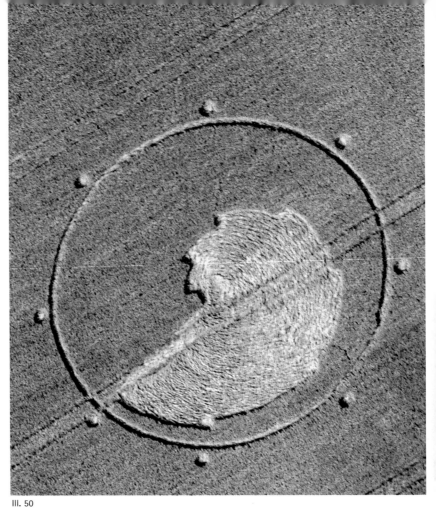
Ill. 50

circle by the different shadings of plants next to the fresh circles. One of the two new formations showed a rectangle inside a circle. The rectangle's surface was finely crisscrossed, creating a grid effect that gave the figure the look of a microchip or, more precisely in this case, a "macrochip" (see Ill. 195). The second formation displayed a six-pointed star with rounded arms "turning" in a counterclockwise direction.

The culmination of the season came on August 8th. Another six-pointed star appeared, similar to the one at Silbury Hill of July 23rd (see Ill. 84) but somewhat smaller at approximately 88 yards (80 m) across (Ill. 96). In the interior of this newer "Koch Star," however, lay another beautiful, flowerlike fractal star. With 198 little circles decorating it, this jewel on Milk Hill, Wiltshire, exhibited a greater number of individual elements

than ever before seen (Ill. 94). The flattened stalks were gathered together in impressive layers displaying complex details (Ill. 95).

Only a day later, on August 9th, another report of a new crop circle came, this time from Etchilhampton. The day before, we had flown over the same field with pilot Graham Slater. Taking note of extensive wind damage, we hadn't considered the field a possible "canvas" for a new formation.

But we had guessed wrong: a 99-yard-long (90 m) key-shaped pictogram lay exactly there (Ill. 97). Seen from the air, the figure was "not very impressive" according to many observers, and so they didn't take the trouble of going into the field when back on the ground. This was unfortunate, because when viewed from the ground the figure displayed many special details (Ills. 98, 99). By the time the formation's unique shapes became known, it was too late for many: the farmer did not allow anyone else into the field. On August 18th came the last

high point of the season, a relatively small figure found at Hackpen Hill, Wiltshire, that closely resembled the "Koch Snowflake," though based on an equilateral triangle (Ill. 102; see also Ill. 129).

Despite these formations, crop circle researchers, spoiled by the pioneering year before, did not consider the 1997 season impressive from the point of view of crop circle numbers or motifs. Fewer than 100 crop circles appeared in England's fields. But without a doubt the country had been blessed again with quite a few "diamonds."

1998: First Seven-sided Figures

The 1998 season in crop circle country started with a bang. On May 4th, a circle 79 yards (72 m) in diameter turned up in a blossoming, shining yellow rape field opposite Silbury Hill (Ill. 100). Thirty-three flame-like elements were lined up evenly one after the other. Although the figure seems relatively simple visually, its geometric construction is unusually complicated. The 33 flames cannot be constructed without the help of

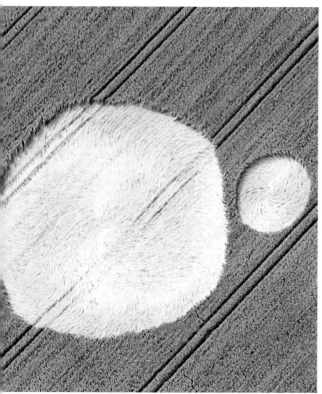

Ill. 51

Ill. 52

47

III. 53

auxiliary circles, which on paper would have to be drawn and then erased. The attempt at a reconstruction by Martin Noakes (Crop Circle Researchers Group, Sussex)[41] shows that this sort of a construction is almost impossible to make in a field (III. 101). Also in 1998, several animal symbols appeared again. On May 25th, the first, a scorpion-like figure, was found near East Kennet, Wiltshire. After that appearance, activity quieted for almost four weeks. Then, on June 20th and 21st, two separate crop circles turned up that fit together like a puzzle. What was flattened in one stood upright in the other and vice

versa (IIIs. 103, 104; see also III. 199). They lay only three miles (5 km) apart, as the crow flies, one at the little town of Marlborough, the other at Furze Hill between Lockeridge and Alton Priors.

A five-pointed star with mandala-like characteristics, as perhaps seen in a medieval cathedral, also appeared on June 20th, in Avebury Trusloe, on the farm of the Butler family (III. 105). When asked the usual questions regarding the circle's origins, Mr. Butler answered diplomatically, as would be expected of a British gentleman: "I know of numerous imitations right here in the Ave-

bury region. But now and again something takes place in the fields, as for example on my land in 1996 (the Triple Julia Set) or again this year as well, which in my opinion cannot be explained with rational logic."

A crop circle 85 yards (77 m) in diameter, reported July 1st in Owslebury, Hampshire, was unusual because of its large, very thin satellite ring (III. 110). Four days later, also in Hampshire at Danebury Hill, there appeared for the first time since people have known about crop circles a seven-sided figure (III. 107). At 48 yards (44 m) in diameter it was certainly no giant, but very harmonious in

III. 53: "The Answer from Roundway," July 26, 1995, 82 yards (74 m)

III. 54: Crop circle near Girten, May 14, 1996

III. 55: "Double Helix," East Field, Alton Barnes, July 17, 1996, 242 yards (220 m) (Photo Steven Alexander)

III. 54

appearance. Constructing a geometrically exact seven-sided figure or seven-pointed star demands great precision. It also requires plotting out a great many auxiliary guidelines to create the final geometric figure.

Only four days later, on July 9th, in the legendary East Field at Alton Barnes, a new highlight followed: again a seven-sided figure, this one 96 yards (87 m) in diameter and decorated with 147 small circles on the outer border. All the circles were flattened in a clockwise direction. The figure's seven-sided edge resembled a saw blade, with seven notches (III. 109; see also III. 125). The rule that every crop circle is exceptional was proven once again, this time by the extraordinarily gentle transitions from flattened to standing grain. We had been watching East Field from the north and south sides the night before without any luck (III. 108). When drizzle and fog arose toward 1 A.M. we gave up, only to stand in astonishment in front of the new formation the next morning. At 6 A.M. we ran into a man driving to work. Arriving at the field soon after that, we could find neither footprints nor any other traces in the soft ground, in spite of the rain the night before. A year later, the formation's silhouette was still easily visible in the new, standing field of grain (III. 106).

The fact that crop circles are not a nuisance for all farmers is evident with the Carsons, who own East Field, with its annual surprises: "We are happy for the crop circles and are thankful that they manifested themselves here so impressively," said the Carsons' older daughter. "We're praying that they will return to our property next year too."

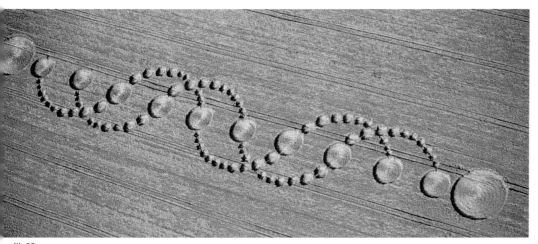

III. 55

Ill. 56: "Julia Set 1,"
Stonehenge, July 7,
1996, 151 circles

Ill. 57: "Julia Set 1"
appeared on Sunday
afternoon between 5:30
and 6!

Ill. 58: At first Farmer
Sandell did not want
anyone in his field. Then
he thought it over. In
the end, around 10,000
curiosity seekers visited
his field.

Ill. 56

III. 57

III. 58

On July 10th, a new, 77-yard-long (70 m) crop circle appeared at West Wood near Lockeridge (III. 111). It was only one of a total of seven formations that turned up in the fields of farmer Fidler at West Overton in 1998.

On July 21st a crop circle 145 yards (132 m) long resembling an animal was discovered in Beckhampton along Highway A4 (III. 113). The "tail" consisted of 53 small circles. Two weeks later another formation joined this one (IIIs. 112, 123). On July 23rd a 94-yard (85 m) square with "spiral corners" (III. 114) appeared on exactly the same spot at Silbury Hill where, on the same date a year earlier, the six-pointed star had been (see IIIs. 84, 191). Distinct layers of flattened wheat characterized the impression of this crop circle (III. 115).

In Rough Down, north of Marlborough, a crop circle appeared only two days later, similar to types that appeared at the beginning of the 1990s (III. 116). Taken as a whole, it was not especially impressive. And the 61 yard (55 m) length of the nine circles of various sizes was relatively modest. But the circles' swirled centers were interesting. The evening before, numerous horse owners had attended a barbecue on the Carter family farm a few hundred yards from the formation. "No one could explain why the horses suddenly began to trot around restlessly in the paddock at 9 P.M.," Mrs. Carter recalls. "There was no reason obvious to us for this." The Carters had had a similar experience eight years earlier and had found a pictogram on their land the next morning.

Another seven-sided geometric form was reported at Upham in Hampshire, where a crop circle had appeared a year before. We took off in search for it with amateur pilot Steve Patterson from the airfield at Thruxton. After a long flight, we finally found the figure: a pretty, small, seven-pointed star. To our surprise, only a bit more than 30 yards (30 m) from the new formation was the shape of the previous year's circle—a somewhat darker, faded, but clearly outlined shadow in the standing grain (IIIs. 73, 74).

On August 2nd, the prehistoric site of Danebury Hill became the showplace of the newest double formation (III. 117). The two figures lay approximately 55 yards (50 m) from one another. This brought to four the number of crop circles in the area (III. 118), since a few days earlier a "Triple Moon" motif had appeared (IIIs. 119, 206). Also in the night of August 2nd an immense configuration 109 yards (99 m) in diameter appeared in the grain fields on the north side of Avebury Ring (Ills. 120 and 2). A quick look from the air showed a relatively simple ring, but when viewed more closely six rounded arches were visible in the flattened wheat (Ill. 121).

A seventh figure appeared at West Woods during the night before August 6th on Fidler's land; it was one of the most impressive of the entire season in England (Ill. 122). New in this one were subtly interwoven or overlapping geometric forms, creating a very complex pattern measuring 88 x 80 yards (80 x 72 m). In the first hours after its discovery several people near the formation experienced problems with their electronic cameras. My camera didn't work either during my first flight over the formation, but only when I was directly over the crop circle. Several hundred yards away it functioned perfectly again. Especially worthy of note is the fact that on the days just before and after August 6th a "forgery team" from the Mitsubishi Corporation had carried out an advertising project for the media, creating the outline of a Mitsuibishi car in East Field, not much more than a mile away (see page 102).

On August 8th the field in Beckhampton where there was already a formation ("The Ray," Ill. 113) became the site of another nighttime creation. The double five-pointed star again exhibited fantastic soft layers with flowing transitions, as though a hairdresser had "styled" the stalks (Ills. 123, 124).

Ill. 59

Ill. 60

Ill. 59: "Moons," Littlebury Green, July 12, 1996 (Photo Ulrich Kox)

Ill. 60: "Circles with Hieroglyphs," Roundway, July 25, 1996

Ill. 61: "Hieroglyphs of Etchilhampton" (compare Ill. 60), 35 yards (32 m)

Ill. 62: "Long Formation of Etchilhampton with Hieroglyphs," July 29, 1996, 1,485 yards (1,350 m)!

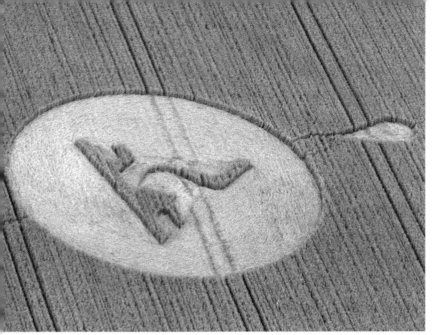

Ill. 61

The showpiece of the seven-sided figures appeared in Tawnsmead Copse on August 9th (Ill. 125). It was like a continuation of the East Field formation (Ill. 109). Beautifully flattened grain was interwoven in this crop circle 138 yards (125 m) in diameter. Each of the 175 small circles decorating the formation was unique, with a center of standing stalks or with swirls, knots, and double knots—an art gallery of varied details (Ills. 126, 127, and 128).

An equilateral triangle, with each side measuring 68 yards (62 m), was discovered on August 10th in Yatesbury, west of Avebury (Ill. 129; see also Ill. 190). In one corner beside three little circles there was an inconspicuous fourth circle, in which only the uppermost parts of the stalks, well above the ground, were swirled. The paths of the stalks in the other formation sections, flattened in

parallel rows with curved transitions to the standing grain, are unique in the history of crop circles (Ill. 130). At Stanton St. Bernhard, Wiltshire, a linseed field also became the canvas for a crop circle on August 16th.

In addition, after the big commotion over these initial August formations was past, other crop circles turned up one at a time here and there in the land as if by magic. Among them was a harmonious figure 110 yards (100 m) in diameter at "Sanctuary" on Highway A4 between Marlborough and Silbury Hill, discovered on August 19 (Ill. 131). The gigantic star of August 25th at Avebury and the triangle at the end of August at Hackpen Hill allowed the season to peter out gently. Of the 190 crop circle formations registered worldwide, around 100 had again turned up in southern England.

Ill. 62

III. 63

1999: The Culmination of the Decade

The experience of past years has shown that each crop circle season arrives with new themes, as far as the basic geometric structure of patterns is concerned. What could be expected in 1999, after the previous year's seven-sided geometry?

The 1999 season began earlier than usual. On April 3rd, in an early-blooming rape field in Wallop near Andover, Hampshire, a finely executed key-shaped pictogram nearly 110 yards (100 m) long was discovered. It resembled the formations of 1990 and 1991.[42] By April 13th, four more formations had appeared at four different locations, according to the Wiltshire Crop Circle Study Group (WCCSG). Among these was an arrangement of five individual circle motifs over 220 yards (200 m) long, which appeared below the white horse of Alton Barnes.[43] So by the end of April, nine figures lay in the fields, although none was particularly impressive visually.

Another crop circle was discovered on May 2nd, again in Wallop, Hampshire. Like the five-circle arrangement at Alton Barnes of April 4th, this one could be associated with the total eclipse of the sun that was to occur on August 11th. That was true for a number of other formations as well.

Also on May 2nd, another crop circle appeared in the same field at Alton Barnes where the April 4th formation occurred. Two crop circles in the same field arising at different times: that is a rarity (III. 132). The new motif represented something com-

pletely unknown and seemed possibly connected to another beautiful symbol found May 23rd at Avebury Trusloe (III. 133). Crop circles had been drawing a lot of attention in this particular field in the past years.

On May 31st, the year's first symbol at Barbury Castle appeared. It closely resembled the Jewish Menorah, the candelabra with seven arms (III. 134). And so that this "oil lamp" should not go out, a pictogram resembling an oil container lay about 55 yards (50 m) away at the same time.

Then, in the night of June 12th, East Field near Alton Barnes—which had been visited annually—had its turn again. Two symbols of gigantic proportions lay 220 yards (200 m) apart in the field (III. 135). One represented a snake motif 187 yards (170 m) long (III. 136). The second crop circle was a stringing together of a well-known motif of the early 1990s. This most complex of all key-shaped pictograms (III. 1) stretched out over 374 yards (340 m).

III. 63: "Creation Symbol," Ashbury, July 26, 1996

III. 64: Stalks from the "Triple Julia Set" bent at the nodes; taken only a few hours after its appearance, thus bending not phototropic (see III. 174).

III. 65: "Triple Julia Set" on Windmill Hill, Avebury, July 29, 1996, 286 x 286 yards (260 x 260 m), 194 circles

III. 64

A peculiarity of several of 1999's formations was that they looked three-dimensional when viewed from the air. The trend started on June 23rd at West Overton, Wiltshire (Ill. 137). What lay in the field seemed like a construction plan for an octahedron, an eight-sided three-dimensional figure with six points. The design consisted of 10 large and 116 small hexagons, all of which could also be viewed as cubes. The 126 individual elements—among which, for the first time, there was not a single circle—also resembled a molecular structure in chemistry.

On the following day the three-dimensional trend continued at Allington: a complex cube in a ball appeared (Ill. 138).

On July 4th, a jewel of a crop circle with a diameter of 149 yards (135 m) lay at the foot of Hackpen Hill (Ill. 139). Represented here in razor-sharp precision was, like many others before it, a figure extremely difficult to construct geometrically, one that would require drawing numerous invisible "plot lines" (Ill. 101). On closer examination this masterpiece demonstrated a puzzling similarity to the Saros cycle, which shows the paths that have been and will be taken by the umbras of various solar eclipses over a span of approximately 1,000 years (Ill. 140). Among those eclipses, of course, was the one to come on August 11, 1999.

A development that had already been hinted at on June 12th in East Field, in "The Snake" with nine coils, was confirmed subsequently. While numerous seven-sided geometric figures had turned up in the previous year, now nine-sided geometric figures were announced. A nine-pointed star was discov-

Ill. 66

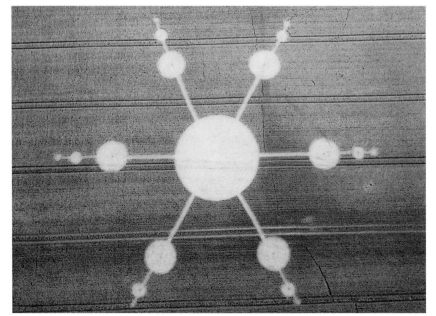

Ill. 67

Ill. 66: "The Double Formation of Liddington," August 2, 1996

Ill. 67: "The Snowflake" of Oliver's Castle, August 11, 1996, see in connection page 114 (Photo Michael Hubbard)

Ill. 68: "Sun Moon Circle" of Liddington

ered on Sugar Hill near Swindon (Ill. 141). The culmination of this development appeared at Cherhill, Wiltshire, on July 18th: a 79-yard (72 m) nine-pointed star that, whether seen from the air or from the ground, reflected the highest aesthetic standards in the formation of its layers and the way its many other details had been carried out (Ill. 9 and photos on cover of the book). Also noteworthy was the proximity of the "White Horse" at Cherhill and the small F-key symbol in a neighboring field, a symbol that has turned up repeatedly on the borders of crop circles. Zecharia Sitchin, a researcher of Sumerian and Old Egyptian symbol writing, has deciphered this F-symbol as a synonym for "The Guardian."[44]

On July 17th, the Butlers' farm once again became a focal point. A gigantic square surrounded by a circle lay at Windmill Hill (Ill. 145; see also Ill. 195). The surface of the square was precisely engraved with 288 small circles, creating a "macrochip."

Two days later. a six-pointed star formation 91 yards (83 m) across appeared in the singularly beautiful rural surroundings of Marlborough Downs. Only persistent negotiating skill kept the angry farmer from mowing down this wondrous work of precision near the prehistoric dolmen at Devil's Den (Ills. 142, 143; see also Ill. 7).

When viewing crop circles from the air it's clear that often the centers of the swirls within the circles are offset from the circles' actual geometric centers. This has been determined in many formations (Ill. 144).

Ill. 69

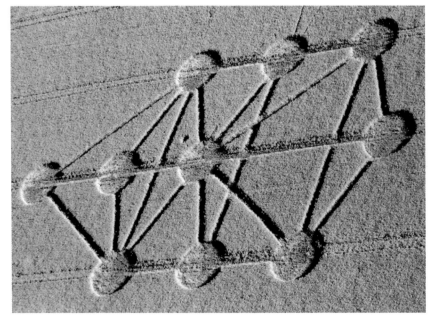

Ill. 70

Ill. 69: "Whirligig with Crescent Moons," Barbury Castle, April 19, 1997, 61 yards (55 m), rape

Ill. 70: "Tree of Life," Burderop Down, May 4, 1997

Ill. 71: "Harlequin Figure," Winterbourne, Bassett, June 1, 1997, barley (Photo Steven Alexander)

Ill. 72: "Snowflake," Stonehenge, June 10, 1997, 149 yards (135 m) (Photo Steven Alexander)

III. 71

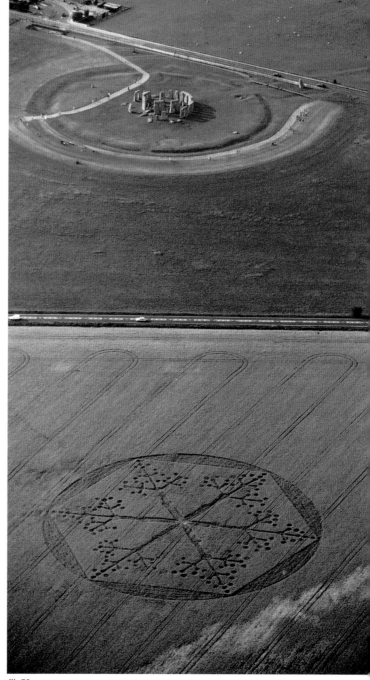

On July 21st, below the prehistoric earthen wall site of Liddington Castle, Farmer Woodtly was again bestowed with a symbol (III. 146). The strange-looking formation had an F-key "signature" similar to the "Cherhill circle" (III. 9). From this field it is approximately a mile (2 km) to the nearest earthen wall site at Barbury Castle, where a simple crop circle easily visible to hikers and walkers appeared on July 23rd (III. 147). Many people thought that the formation's three interlocking crescent moons resembled dolphins (III. 151).

Five more formations in southern England were discovered on July 23rd, and on the following day people were drawn to another new formation at Silbury Hill (III. 148; see also Ills. 3, 187). A classic fractal geometric figure lay 110 yards (100 m) from Europe's largest pyramid, in a field at Firthfarm. A mile west of that, a six-sided "looped band," also called a "Celtic Knot" (III. 149), emerged in the night of July 28th.

Although the farmer at Firthfarm had been cool with us the year before, he proved friendlier this time and even drove us in his Land Rover to the field in question. But he did grumble to himself repeatedly: "They should keep their hands off my farm!" When asked

III. 72

whom he meant by "they," he admitted, surprising himself, "I don't actually know."

On July 31st, "The Crown," the gigantic formation described in part I of this book, appeared at Roundway Hill (Ills. 4, 6, 8). The site of an ancient burial mound, the Long Barrow of West Kennet, was the seat of activity on August 4th. Again there was a fractal geometric figure based upon a square; the formation totaled 120 yards (109 m) across. Each component square was divided into triangles (Ill. 150). A very noticeable detail was a large, blossoming thistle exactly in the center of standing grain in one of the formation's 120 small circles; very few thistles could be found in the surrounding field (Ill. 152). Moreover, the little "thistle circle" lay precisely at its own spot, just as did the 199 other circles without thistles.

Next came a new sensation at Bishops Cannings. Toward the end of a nighttime reconnaissance tour, in the early morning hours of August 6th, the German crop circle researcher Andreas Müller discovered a type of crop circle construction never before found. Our earlier experience with the field's owners had been so unpleasant that we decided to investigate the field first without the farmer's permission. In the center of the middle circle of the figure, which had seven axes, were seven stalks of grain still standing (Ill. 153). The decision to search spontaneously for the figure in the field had been the right one. Only an hour and a half after its discovery, farmer Nolton mowed down the work of art in his field. "What is taking place in the fields is pure vandalism," he shouted at a group of horrified onlookers.

What he called "vandalism" is shown in illustration 157, an aerial photograph. Miraculously, a crop circle enthusiast from the lower Rhine in Germany, Ulrich Kox, took several aerial photos of the circle. He was actually on the way to another formation when he flew over the new crop circle by chance. Not only was the relatively small symbol extremely precisely laid out, but the flattened figure's entire structure was a single perfectly interlaced woven form (Ill. 154). In spite of its short life span it has been dubbed unforgettably as "The Basket" in the history of crop circles. Apparently Farmer Nolton could not bear the fact that he had received this "basket." "It was as though he had scratched an eye out of the earth"

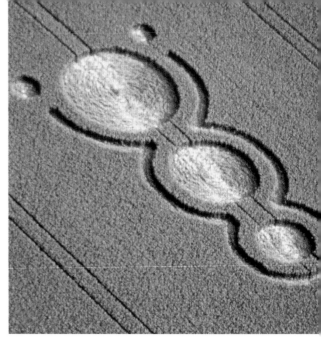

Ill. 73

Ill. 74

Ill. 75

Ill. 76

Ill. 73: "The Earth Goddess," Upham, June 15, 1997 (Photo Ron Russell

Ill. 74: "Silhouette of the Earth Goddess" of 1997, with "Seven-pointed Star" of 1998 (see page 51)

Ill. 75: Crop circle southeast of Winchester, July 6, 1997, 33 yards (30 m), barley

Ill. 76: "Quinta Essentia," Headbourne Worthy (see page 125), July 7, 1997, 94 yards (85 m), wheat

wrote the Swiss journalist Balz Theus in a report, which otherwise was written in a cynical tone and also proved to contain mistakes.[45] In 1999, as in years preceding, several crop circle formations were destroyed before they could be studied carefully (Ill. 155; see also Ill. 88). What had begun early ended late: On September 1st a beautiful "flower" with eight axes appeared in the wheat at Manor Farm at Avebury. The 148th and last figure of the 1999 crop circle year in southern England was a simple circle located not, as usual, in wheat, but in corn.

2000 and 2001: The New Millenium

Neither the year 2000 nor 2001 was comparable with 1999. Nevertheless in the summer of 2000 144 crop circles appeared in England. Most weren't up to the standards of 1999's figures, with two exceptions: the mid-July formation named "Magnetic Field" and the beautifully perfected "Logarithm Spirals" of August 13th. Both appeared in Wiltshire. Ninety figures were recorded in England in 2001. Many were fakes. But on August 12th the "Flower of Milk Hill" in Wiltshire brought new dimensions: consist-

ing of 409 circles, this overpowering figure surprised even the most confirmed skeptics. It measured 275 yards (250 m) in diameter and resembled 1996's "Julia Set" (see Ill. 65).

A Look beyond England

Without question crop circles appear most frequently in the south of England. But numerous circles and formations have been discovered in many other countries and particularly in the Netherlands, Germany, the United States, Canada, and the Czech Republic.

61

The first dated sighting outside England occurred in 1966: six circles were discovered in a sugar beet field at Tully, in Queensland, Australia. A television reporter from Sydney made aerial photos of them. The stalks were flattened in a circular form and partially uprooted. Because no one had an explanation for this formation, which was approximately 11 yards (10 m) across, the circles were called "UFO Nests." A little later three other circles were found not far from the first.[46] In 1972, an 11-yard (10 m) circle at Loughuile in Ireland; a concentric double ring 17 yards (15 m) in diameter at Hiortkvam near Örebro in Sweden; and a 10-yard (9 m) circle at Wellington, New Zealand, were reported. Farmer Edwin Fuhr discovered five circles and a ring in a grain field near Langenbury in the Canadian province of Saskatchewan in 1974. And in 1977 a whole series of circles was reported in Australia.

At the beginning of the 1990s the leap noted in England in the number and complexity of crop circles was reflected worldwide. In 1990 alone there were 60 circles reported in the United States, with the largest concentration in Missouri and Kansas. In Canada, 25 circles were reported. In addition circles were found in Europe, for example in the Netherlands.[47] In more recent years the number of sightings in Canada—around 20 to 30 a year—has remained constant, while reports from the U.S. have decreased sharply. Only six formations were reported in 1999. The Czech Republic, on the other hand, moved more to center stage with about a dozen formations, some of them very impressive, reported each year

III. 77

since 1997. (1999's figures were more modest, though.)[48]

The Netherlands and Germany

In no other country apart from England have so many crop circles appeared since 1986 as in the Netherlands. From 1986 to 1999, 151 discoveries were registered. In the 10 years from 1986 to 1995 there were 47 all together. Then in 1996 alone there were 44 formations, among which were keylike pictograms resembling those sighted in England in 1990. Following that, the number dropped to 33 in 1997 and 11 in 1998. There were 16 crop circles again in 1999. What is striking about the Netherlands' crop circle history is that simple grass circles have been discovered in the middle of winter.[49]

III. 77: "The Torus," Alton Barnes, July 11, 1997, 110 yards (100 m)

III. 78: Details from "The Torus"; stalks flattened, as though arranged by a hairdresser

III. 79: "Hopi Star," Bishops Cannings, July 13, 1997, 61 yards (55 m)

III. 78

In 1991, a year later than in England, circle fever broke out in Germany. It literally took off at the end of May with a double circle at Idstein and another at Felm in mid-July. Both proved to have been trampled down by nocturnal pranksters in the fields. By the middle of August, a total of 26 formations had been reported in Germany. Several of them displayed beauty and precision comparable to the English examples.

A large and complicated pictogram that appeared in Grasdorf near Hildesheim on July 23rd aroused the greatest interest (Ill. 156).

It was around 110 yards (100 m) long and 33 yards (30 m) wide and consisted of seven symbols and 13 circles, a formation reminiscent of an ancient sun symbol. News of the Grasdorf pictogram's discovery spread throughout Germany and beyond. Thousands of curious people found their way to the formation, seemingly repeating the scenes of throngs in England's East Field the previous year. A treasure seeker using a metal detector claims to have found three massive plates of bronze, silver, and gold beneath three of the Grasdorf formation's circles. All had relieflike symbols on them identical to the symbol in the field. Today two of the plates, the bronze and the silver, are said to be in the hands of an industrialist. The golden one has disappeared. The plates were shown in public on several occasions. The German Federal Institute for Materials Research and Testing certified a very high metallurgical purity. One can only speculate about the actual source and measure of truth of the entire story, since neither the

III. 81

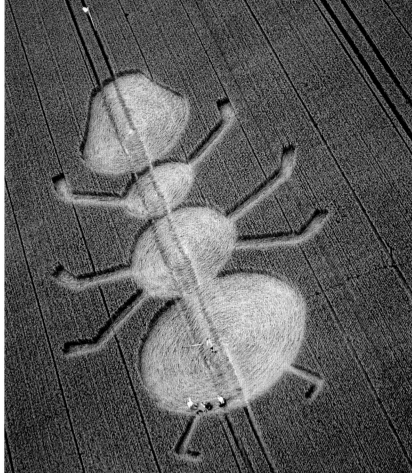

III. 82

name of the person who found them nor the name of the owner is known.

It was quieter in 1992 in Germany, just as it was in England. But even in this year several formations turned up. One of them was directly on the Swiss border in Eschen, on the road leading to Nendeln. Swissair pilot Ferdinand Schmid had seen the three circles, connected by lines, from the air and visited them shortly thereafter. In 1993, among other formations, a pictogram was discovered near the Swiss border, this time in the administrative district of Waldshut.[50]

New crop circles also appeared in Germany in subsequent years. A series of 12 formations found in the state of Schleswig-Holstein in the summer of 1996 was especially noteworthy. Four of the configurations were similar to the key-shaped pictograms of Wiltshire in 1990. In 1997 as well, the focal point of crop circle activity was in Schleswig-Holstein, with 10 of the 16 formations reported in all of Germany (III. 158); in 1998, 15 of the year's 24 formations were reported in that area.

In 1999 only eight crop circles were recorded, this time with most reported in Hesse. Two of the six "Hessian" formations were discovered on June 26th at Ehlen, not far from Kassel. According to information from observer Wolfgang Schöppe, one formation, a very impressive wavy spiral, had appeared during the day. He had driven by at 8 in the morning on Highway A4, from which the spiral was easily visible later, without noticing anything unusual. Then, at 4 P.M., the formation was discovered by another driver (III. 159a). The other impressive and quite large formation displayed four "claws," a ring, and eight circles (III. 159b).[51]

And Switzerland?

Little is known of any crop circles in Switzerland. A few dozen small groups of three are said to have been found in the area of Zurich Oberland in 1975 and 1976, primarily in forest clearings and grassy areas. Several people said of these that they could be the landing tracks of UFOs.[52]

On June 18, 1993, in the Saane Valley near Gümmenen, close to Bern, a crop circle was discovered that created a considerable stir in the Swiss press (Ill. 160). Since it lay in a green wheat field directly alongside a railway viaduct on the stretch of railroad between Neuenberg and Bern, thousands of train travelers had a very good bird's-eye view of it. Thomas Peterlunger photographed the little key pictogram, searched for suspicious tracks, took samples of wheat (Ill. 161; see also Ill. 173) and questioned the farmers who worked the field. The figure was relatively modest at 20 yards (18.4 m) long, with a circle 13 yards (11.5 m) in diameter.

"What I find especially interesting is the fact that this Swiss circle triggered the entire phenomenon of English crop circle research," Thomas Peterlunger wrote, "along with mixed reactions from the press, twisting of facts, and ridicule of those who tried to come to terms with the phenomenon seriously." In contrast to Peter Marthaler and his wife—the farmers involved—Thomas Peterlunger believes that "the Gümmenen circle is not some trick of a nocturnal prankster." He supports this idea by citing, among other things, his observations of grain-stalk samples: "The seeds taken from

III. 83

the interior of the circle seemed dried out to a certain extent. They were smaller, lighter than samples taken outside the circle and showed irregular malformations that were seldom present in seeds from wheat that wasn't part of the formation" (Ill. 176).[53] After this well-researched and controversial case, crop circle activity in Switzerland was quiet for the next five years.

Then, at the beginning of 1998, Emil Neff of Appenzell, Switzerland, found a puzzling symbol in his grassland. Small yet conspicuous, two touching circles lay in the grassland in the form of a figure eight.

Also at the beginning of 1998, Swiss farmer Jakob Thalmann discovered on his land in Homberg in Aargau a small wheat circle with a concentric ring around it. He too formed his opinion quickly: "Clearly an act of vandalism!" And his son Markus Thalmann had the same opinion: "That was only the doing of a couple of crazy people. After all, there is a full moon."[54]

The Swiss media, however, in recent years has followed crop circle events abroad with increasing interest and astonishing impartiality.

Similar Phenomena Cause Sensations

It's true that relatively few crop circles have been discovered in Switzerland, but another phenomenon in the 1980s and early 1990s in the area around Lake Geneva in western Switzerland repeatedly created a sensation: the sudden appearance of circular holes in the ground. What sounds at first like an absurd joke is highly puzzling on second look.

In 1972, in Echallens on the farm of the farmer Mertinat, near a stall for young cattle, a circular hole 2 yards (2 m) in diameter and 5 feet (1.5 m) deep appeared. One-hundred fifty-eight cubic feet (4.5 m³) of earth had disappeared. Nine years later, on the morning of December 5, 1981, a second hole was discovered. A cylindrical cavity 26.4 feet (8 m) deep and 6 yards (5 m) across was found

III. 83: A recurring phenomenon: A large number of plants in the flattened area remain untouched and standing beside many changed stalks.

III. 84: Fractal star, Silbury Hill, July 23, 1997, 99 yards (90 m), 126 circles; a year later, another crop circle appeared in this same place (Ill. 187)

III. 85: Fractal star diagram (Andreas Müller)

III. 84

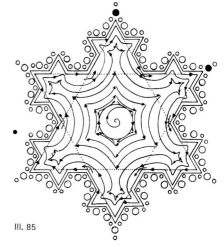

III. 85

between Ollon and Villars in the hamlet of Les Combes, not far from the vacation home of Claude Chapuis, an airline pilot. Some 5,495 cubic feet (157 m³) of "excavated material" was missing. Almost exactly a year later, on December 17, 1982, the farmer Roland Häfeli stood puzzled in front of yet another such hole. It measured 6 yards (5.5 m) in diameter and 25 feet (7.5 m) deep. Every trace of 6,230 cubic feet (178 m³) of earth was missing.

But by far the largest mysterious hole developed during the night between February 3rd and 4th, in a community on the outskirts of Geneva. The chasm lay in a large field with winter plantings, had a diameter of 11 yards (10 m) and was 40 feet (12 m) deep. Missing were 32,970 cubic feet (942 m³) of earth, or about 2,000 tons of material.

One hundred trucks would have had to be loaded with 20 tons each to haul away this material. According to published descriptions, the excavated material literally disappeared; nothing pointed to any trace of heavy vehicles having transported the earth away, and area residents had not reported any unusual happenings or noise.

Common to all these holes was the fact that they were "cut out" in a circle. And in none were there traces of vegetation, which would have been the case if there had been a normal sinking of the ground.

These descriptions must certainly be read with care. It was not possible for the authors of this book to investigate the reports given.

In July 1998, on the other side of the world, the appearance of a gigantic figure in the sand in Australia's outback drew attention (Ill. 163). The figure, which became known as the "Marree Man," lay on a remote plateau 36 miles (60 km) west of the small town of Marree and portrayed a naked Aborigine. The image was so gigantic, with its length of 2.4 miles (4 km), that satellite pictures could have easily been made of it. How the Marree Man was plowed into the sparse desert earth remains disputed. Every line of the figure is 39 yards (35 m) wide. "In order to 'draw' the entire outline with a plough, a single tractor would have had to travel hundreds of miles," the Australian daily newspaper *The West Australian* estimated in its November 4, 1998, edition. "The inhabitants of Marree assure us in addition that they had no idea who created the figure, although to create such a well-proportioned figure high-tech equipment would have been necessary." Within six months the figure had disappeared due to the effects of weather.

Another phenomenon—snow circles—is mentioned in Michael Hesemann's book, *Crop Circles.* According to researcher Colin Andrews, wrote Hesemann, a team of geologists from Cambridge University discovered approximately 30 "crop circles of great variety in the deep snow" in the highlands of Afghanistan on an expedition in 1990. Prior to that, in 1975, "snow circles" had appeared in Anatolia, a part of Turkey.

"Ice circles" have been documented in photographs. Photos from Canada and Scandinavia show slowly rotating, perfectly rounded ice floes several dozen yards in diameter. Academic science has explained their origin as due to the conditions in slow-flowing river waters.

Ill. 86

Ill. 86: Formation at Oliver's Castle (same site as "Triple Moon," 1994, Ill. 31), July 23, 1997, 77 yards (70 m)

Ill. 87: Bends at the growth nodes of stalks flattened in a clockwise direction, Oliver's Castle circle (see also Ill. 174)

Ill. 88: When a third crop circle appeared in his field in early August 1997, Farmer Woodtly got out his thresher.

Ill. 89: A destroyed circle. Farmer Woodtly was not favorably disposed to crop circles.

Ill. 90: The answer to Farmer Woodtly's act of vandalism: new circles on his farm at the foot of Liddington Castle.

Ill. 91: A precise arch between circles is difficult to create mechanically because the centers of the circles are so far apart.

Ill. 87

Ill. 88

Ill. 90

Ill. 89

Ill. 91

69

Ill. 92

Ill. 93

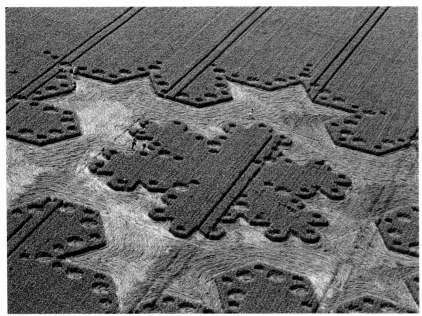

Ill. 94

Ill. 95

Ill. 92: "Mickey Mouse," Vernham Dean, end of July 1997

Ill. 93: Double formation, Etchilhampton, August 2, 1997

Ill. 94: Low aerial photo of the star at Milk Hill, an especially beautiful location

Ill. 95: Star detail (Diagram Andreas Müller)

Ill. 96: Fractal star, Milk Hill, Alton Barnes, August 8, 1997, 88 yards (80 m), 198 circles

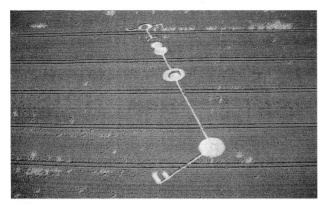

III. 97

III. 98

III. 99

III. 100

Ill. 97: Key-shaped pictogram, Etchilhampton, August 9, 1997, 99 yards (90 m)

Ill. 98: Detail of the key symbol: gentle transitions with rounded edges

Ill. 99: Detail of the key symbol: These crescent moons have "soft" corners as well.

Ill. 100: "Beltan Wheel," West Kennet Long Barrow, May 4, 1998, 79 yards (72 m), rape

Ill. 101: Diagram of the "Beltan Wheel," according to Martin Noakes not possible to construct in the field

Ill. 102: Fractal at Hackpen Hill, August 18, 1997 (Photo Steven Alexander)

Ill. 103: Creation symbol at Clatford, June 20, 1998, 66 yards (60 m), barley

Ill. 104: Creation Symbol at Furze Hill, June 21, 1998 (see Ill. 103)

Ill. 101

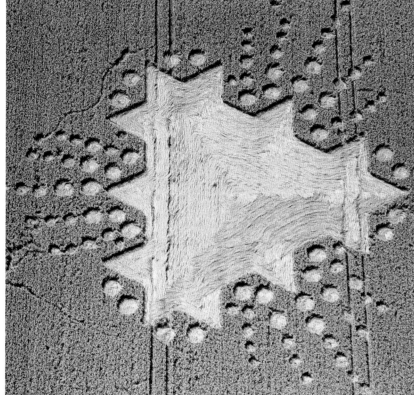

Ill. 102

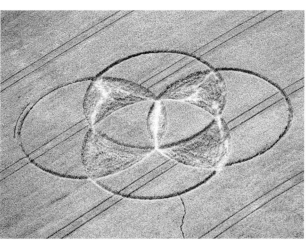

Ill. 103

Ill. 104

Ill. 105

Ill. 106

Ill. 107

Ill. 108

Ill. 105: Five-pointed star at Avebury Truesloe, June 20, 1998, 85 yards (77 m), wheat

Ill. 106: Shadow image remaining a year after appearance of sevenfold geometric figure at East Field (see Ill. 109 and pages 107 ff.)

Ill. 107: Sevenfold geometry at Danebury Hill, July 5, 1998, 48 yards (44 m), wheat

Ill. 108: We had conducted a night watch on the north and south sides of this field until 1 A.M. The crop circle was discovered at 6:15 A.M. after a rainy night.

Ill. 109: Sevenfold geometry, East Field at Alton Barnes, July 9, 1998, 96 yards (87 m), 147 circles

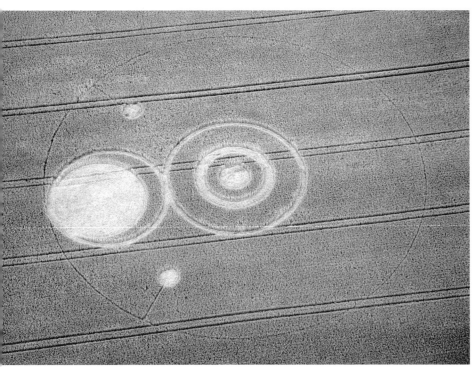

III. 110

III. 111

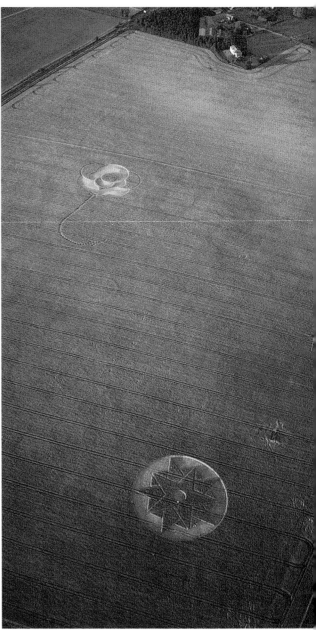

III. 112

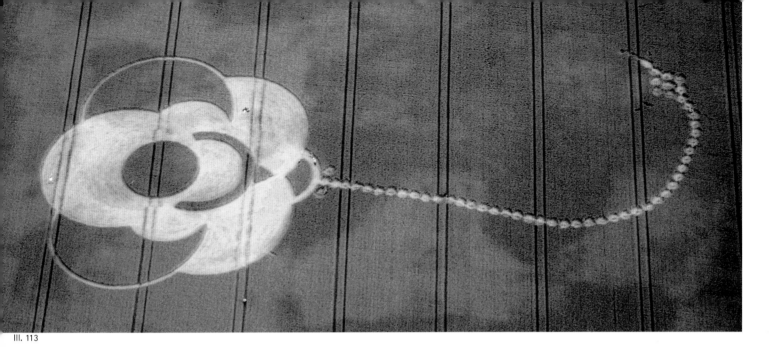

Ill. 113

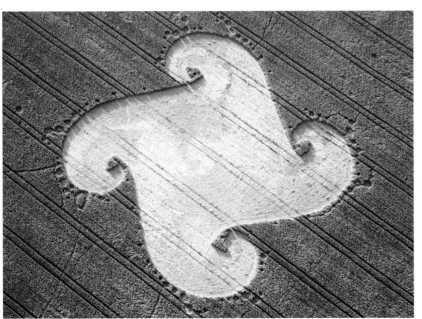

Ill. 114

Ill. 115

77

III. 116

III. 117

III. 118

Ill. 119

Ill. 116: Circles in Rough
Down, July 25, 1998.
Had horses sensed the
circles' creation?

Ill. 117: Double
formation at Danebury
Hill, August 2, 1998

Ill. 118: The four crop
circles in the vicinity of
Danebury Hill: July 5,
end of July, and August
2, 1998

Ill. 119: "Triple Moon,"
near Danebury Hill, end
of July 1998

Ill. 120: Ring with
decorative arcs at
Avebury, August 2,
1998, 109 yards (99 m)

Ill. 121: Diagram by
Andreas Müller

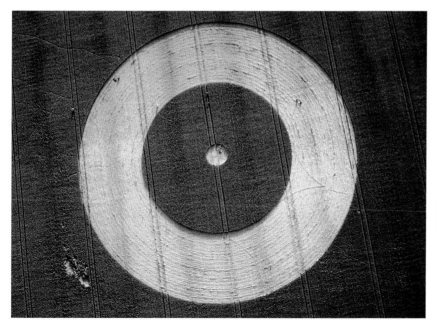

Ill. 120

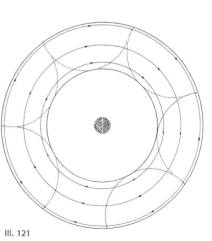

Ill. 121

79

Ill. 123

Ill. 124: "The Queen" of West Wood, August 6, 1998. Several people experienced electromagnetic disturbances with their cameras.

Ill. 123: Five-pointed star, Beckhampton, August 8, 1998, 70 yards (64 m)

Ill. 124: Detail of the star at Beckhampton. The edge on the right side of the path is rounded off.

Ill. 125: Seven-sided figure at Tawnsmead Copse, August 9, 1998, 138 yards (125 m). The design elaborated on the sevenfold figure at East Field (Ill. 109).

Ill. 125

Ill. 126

Ill. 127

Ill. 128

Ill. 129

Ill. 126: Detail of one of the interiors of a "nest," one of 175 small circles

Ill. 127: 175 unique small circles created a crop circle gallery; this "nest" had a standing stalk in the middle.

Ill. 128: Diagram of seven-sided figure (Ill. 125) by Andreas Müller

Ill. 129: Triangle, Yatesbury, August 10, 1998, 68 yards (62 m)

Ill. 130: Detail from Yatesbury triangle; layers of grain at the edge form an arch into the standing grain.

Ill. 131: Crop circle at Sanctuary, August 19, 1998, 110 yards (100 m) (Photo Francine Blake)

Ill. 132: "Phases of the Eclipse of the Sun," Milk Hill at Alton Barnes, April 4, 1999, blossoming rape. In the same field another crop circle appeared on May 2 (on the right in the photo). (Photo Francine Blake)

Ill. 133: "Flower" of Avebury Trusloe, May 23, 1999

Ill. 130

Ill. 131

Ill. 132

Ill. 133

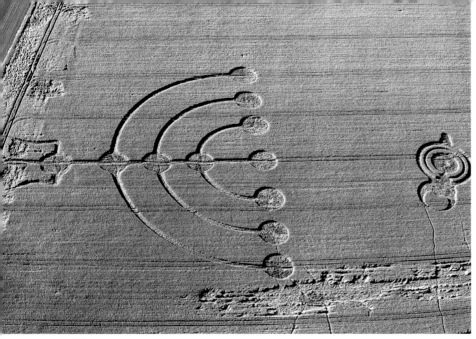

III. 134

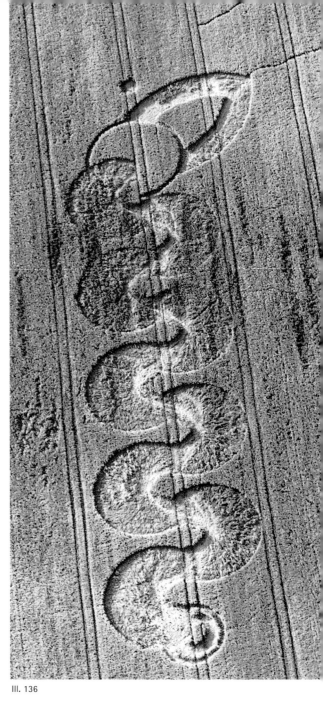

III. 135

III. 136

III. 137

III. 134: "Candelabra with Seven Arms" of Barbury Castle, also called "Menorah," May 31, 1999

III. 135: Double formation in East Field, June 12, 1999

III. 136: "The Snake" in East Field, June 12, 1999, 187 yards (170 m)

III. 137: "Octahedron Model," West Overton, June 23, 1999. The 126 individual parts were all hexagons; crop circles without circular elements are rare.

III. 138: "The Escher Cube" of Allington, three dimensions in the field, June 24, 1999

III. 138

Ill. 139

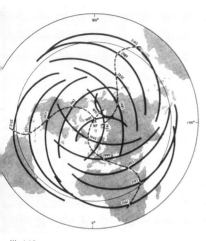

Ill. 140

Ill. 139: "Saros Cycle" at
Hackpen Hill, July 4,
1999, 149 yards (135 m).
Like the Beltan Wheel's,
this crop circle's
geometry is virtually
impossible to construct
in the field.

Ill. 140: Diagram of
"Saros Cycle": Over the
course of 1,000 years
the umbras of the sun's
eclipses move across the
planets according to this
scheme.

Ill. 141: Nine-pointed
star at Sugar Hill near
Swindon, June 24, 1999

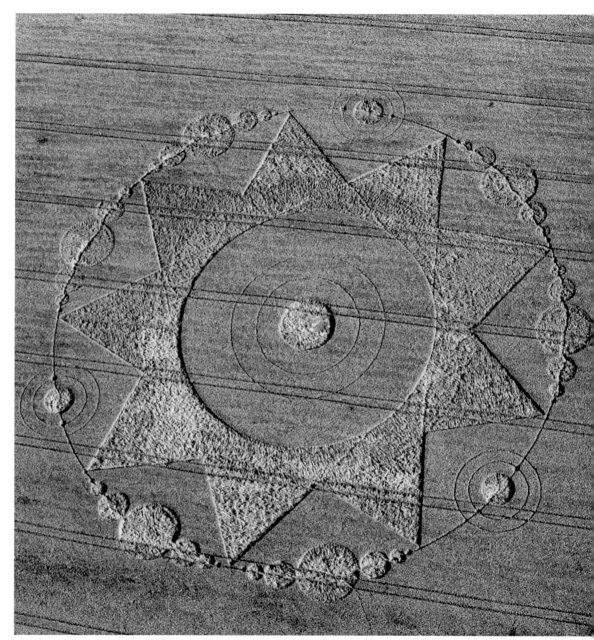

Ill. 141

Ill. 142

Ill. 143

Ill. 142: Six-pointed star near the dolmen at Devil's Den, July 19, 1999

Ill. 143: Whoever reaches a new crop circle first has the chance to see undisturbed and interesting details. Left to right: Janet Ossebaard and Bert Janssen from Holland and Frank Laumen from Germany.

Ill. 144: The centers of the radially flattened swirls are offset from the circles' geometric centers.

Ill. 145: "The Macrochip" of Windmill Hill, Avebury, July 17, 1999, 288 small circles

Ill. 144

Ill. 146: Strange motif at Liddington Castle, July 21, 1999, with F-key as at Cherhill

Ill. 147: "Crescent Moon" at the wall of Burbury Castle (a favorite destination for excursions), July 23, 1999

Ill. 148: Fractal geometry at Silbury Hill, July 24, 1999

Ill. 149: "The Celtic Knot" at Beckhampton, July 28, 1999, 79 yards (72 m)

Ill. 150: Fractal geometry at the Long Barrow of West Kennet, August 4, 1999, 120 yards (109 m)

Ill. 147

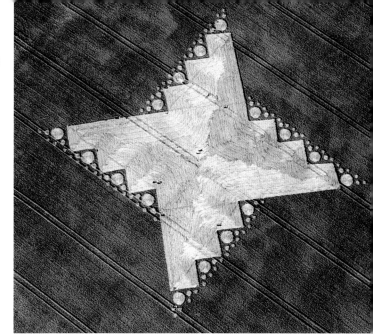

Ill. 148

Ill. 149

Ill. 150

Ill. 151

Ill. 153

Ill. 151: Others named this crop circle "The Dancing Dolphins"; 75 yards (68 m), wheat

Ill. 152: Blossoming thistle standing in the center of one of the 120 small circles (see Ill. 150)

Ill. 153: Detail from "The Basket": seven standing stalks in the center circle of a seven-sided figure (see Ill. 157)

Ill. 154: Detail of woven layers of grain, discovered by Andreas Müller during our early tour (see Ill. 157)

Ill. 152

Ill. 154

93

III. 155

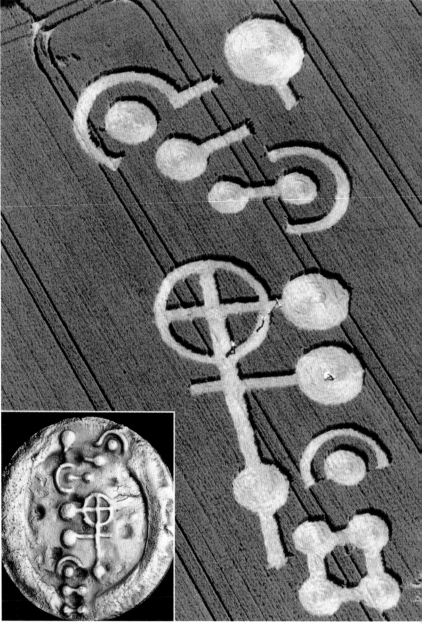

III. 155: Farmer vandalism: this mowed path led to "The Basket," a quantum leap in crop circle construction, two hours after its discovery.

III. 156: Grasdorf pictograms near Hildesheim, June 23, 1991 (Photo Michael Hesemann)

III. 157: "The Basket" at Bishops Cannings, August 6, 1999: basketry as a new method of circle creation! A hint of circles to come? (Photo Ulrich Kox)

III. 156

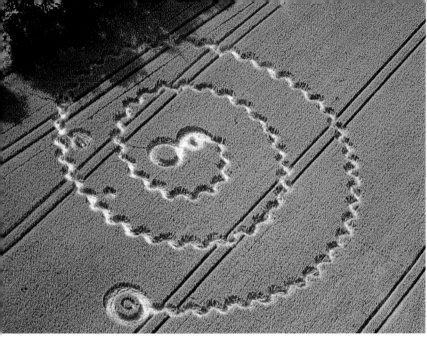

Ill. 159a

Ill. 160

Ill. 159b

Ill. 158: Labyrinth at Burghasungen near Kassel, June 29, 1997 (Photo Ulrich Kox)

Ill 159a: "The Spiral" at Ehlen in Hesse, June 26, 1999, (Photo Ulrich Kox)

Ill. 159b: "The Claw" at Ehlen, June 26, 1999, (Photo Ulrich Kox)

Ill. 160: "The Key" of Gümmenen, Bern, June 18, 1993 (Photo Thomas Peterlunger)

Ill. 161: Thickening of a grain stalk node in the "Gümmenen Key" (Photo Thomas Peterlunger)

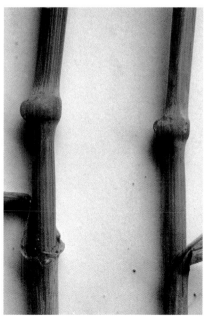

Ill. 161

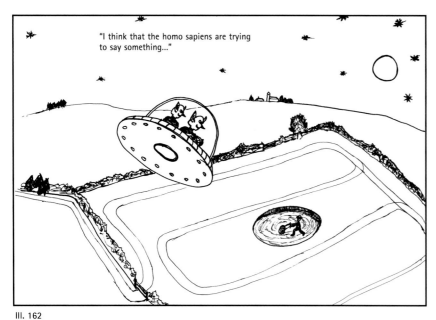

III. 162

"Now it's starting to happen on my carpet too!"

III. 164

III. 163

III. 162: Cartoon by Werner Anderhub

III. 163: Sand picture in the Australian desert, discovered in July 1998, satellite photo. The 2.4-mile-long (4 km) "Marree Man" created excitement worldwide.

III. 164: Cartoon based on an idea by Olson

III The Search for
Causes and Creators

Which Is "Fake" and Which Is "Authentic?"

"As far as the natives here in Wiltshire County are concerned, the majority opinion is that the crop circles are not made by human hands." Janet Parr is convinced of that. "But that doesn't change the city folk who come here from London year after year and tell us that it's not so," she says. "They always think they know everything better than we do, and then publish the same nonsense ideas in the media." The elderly inhabitant of Alton Barnes gets passionate when talking about it: "There's simply no explanation why these types of complex structures are created in our fields—often several in one night—in a very short period of time." The farmers don't have the time to make something like that, she adds as a further argument. And they wouldn't harm their own grain. For this elderly woman it is clear: "Anyone who doesn't want to believe that something supernatural is taking place here is simply narrow-minded."

For farmer Polly Carson, also, there is no question that many crop circle formations were not made by human hands. Carson's

East Field at Alton Barnes has become world famous since 1990, with spectacular formations appearing year after year.

For that reason the Carsons are repeatedly accused of creating the figures themselves or of giving the job to "forgers" in order to draw numerous curiosity seekers to their fields. Polly Carson reacts indignantly to these accusations and at the same time laughs: "We'd never be able to create anything so perfectly beautiful!" There have been "fakes" in their fields, Carson says, but "they were very easy to tell from the other figures because of their shabby construction. They cause us great offense." (Ill. 165; see also Ills. 34, 200)

John Tobin, a retiree from neighboring Stanton St. Bernard, sees things entirely differently: "Nothing much happens out here in the summer. So young people go out into the fields and carry on all sorts of nonsense to attract the attention of the public and earn some money. It's the silly season!" The British army, he goes on to say, has proven that the circles in the grain fields can be created in a matter of minutes with a garden roller or using boards.

Even amateur pilot Steve Patterson is convinced that "these wonderful crop circle configurations are all created by humans." The big question that bothers him is, "What causes people to put such fantastic, transitory works of art in grain fields?" For Patterson, the real inexplicable phenomenon is "the mysterious power that directs these human crop circle creators to work so very precisely." The Briton has seen and carefully photographed many crop circles from the air

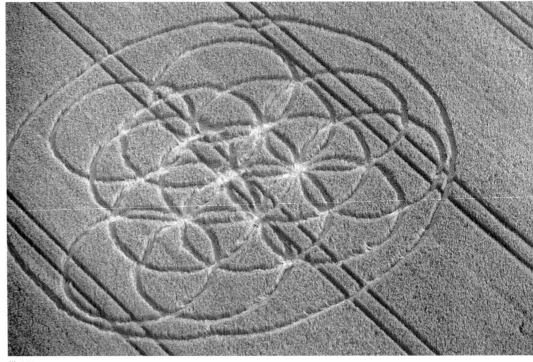

Ill. 165

but concedes that he has "very seldom" visited a crop circle on foot, to look more carefully at its composition from the ground.

The discussion whether crop circles are "authentic"—in other words, truly "supernatural" phenomenon—or "fakes" made by humans is as old as the first media reports about them, which started in the early 1980s. Ever since, the debate has continued between "believers" and "skeptics."

"The use of the term 'fake' must have logically come because of something 'authentic' before it," Andy Thomas ruminates in his book, *Vital Signs*. "Were there

ever really 'fakes'?"[55] There were, insofar as you can equate "fake" with "man-made." It has been proven dozens of times that every summer in England a whole lot of figures made by humans appear in grain (Ill. 166). Sometimes the forgers are caught or observed at their nighttime activities. Some openly create figures for various experimental purposes or for commercial enterprise.

This has already happened on behalf of television stations and the print media as well as private firms for the purpose of advertising.

Ill. 165: "Wilted Tree of Life" in East Field at Alton Barnes, July 1997; obviously, an interrupted job by beginners

Ill. 166: Man-made fractal at Rockley, July 10, 1999. The tracks of a trampler were very obvious in the standing grain.

Ill. 167: "Experimental Circle" by the Germans Koch and Kyborg at Woodborough Hill, July 1997

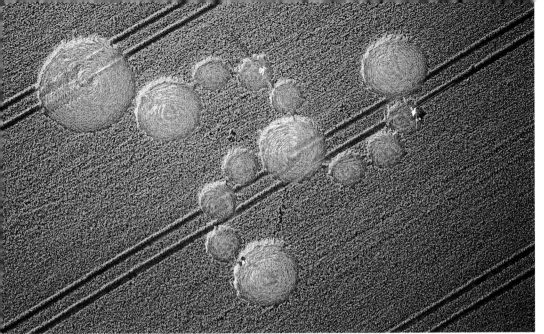

III. 166

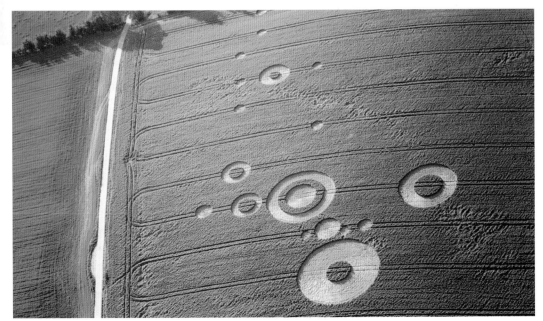

III. 167

Task: "Faking" Circles

Joachim Koch and Hans-Jürgen Kyborg are among those people who pay farmers for permission to create figures in the fields. They stress that their "experimental" formations shouldn't be considered "fakes" (III. 167). Their motive is to establish contact via pictograms with the "non-human intelligence" they believe is behind the "authentic" crop circles. In the summer of 1999 they were already at work in the field at Woodborough Hill at Alton Barnes for the ninth time. Both are convinced that they have actually succeeded in establishing contact with this intelligence. Moreover, they claim to have received "sensational information" from the large pictograms of the early 1990s "about a stellar system near the sun in which life can exist." In their book *The Answer of Orion* they present the length and breadth of their supposed new discoveries on 300 pages.[56]

At the beginning of the 1990s, a group with the name "The United Bureau of Investigation" tried to come in contact with the unknown intelligence by making grain formations.

While people like Koch and Kyborg puttered around with their own thing, there were also private firms that hired known forgers to create logos or other commercial designs in the fields. Along these lines the logos of two British pop bands were placed in grain fields in Long Marston, Warwickshire on July 7, 1995 and July 16, 1997.[57]

On August 5 and 6, 1998, the forgery team known as the "CircleMakers" (they called themselves "Team Satan" before then) was at work in East Field for the Japanese automotive firm Mitsubishi. Even though they could work in safety and in daylight on the advertising project, thanks to the permission of farmer Tim Carson, they needed two days to complete the outline of the Mitsubishi car (Ill. 168). During the very night between their two work days (the night before August 6th) one of the most complex crop circles of the 1998 season turned up little more than a mile away from the "Mitsubishi" (see Ill. 122). Would the three "CircleMakers," John Lundberg, Geoff Gilbertson, and Rod Dickinson, have immediately worked through another night between two days of strenuous work out of sheer enthusiasm, to fabricate another, highly polished "hoax?"

Additional man-made crop circles were created practically every year in the 1990s at the behest of TV stations and newspapers. Among them were several that, seen from the air, were very impressive. In the night before July 26, 1998, the "CircleMakers" and the well-known forger Doug Bower created two formations for the British television network BBC at the foot of Milk Hill (Ill. 169). To the consternation of many, two UFO researchers, the Britons Matthew Williams and Paul Daimon, caught the BBC hoaxers in the act of making the figures in the early evening. John Lundberg's team created a complex-looking fractal that was actually based on a simple construction plan. At the same time, the sprightly retiree Bower was busy making a large, simple circle with three

III. 168

smaller "satellites" at the same time. The short night was not sufficient to complete it. Both figures, whose "creation" the BBC filmed at night with infrared cameras, had to be finished in the daylight.[58]

Even before the 1998 circle year had begun in the northern hemisphere, the much-sought-after "Team Satan" was active. At the request of the American NBC television network, Lundberg, Dickinson, and Russell were brought to a remote area near Winton on the south island of New Zealand at the beginning of March—late summer there—to create a fractal formation.[59] Money apparently did not play a role. The event was broadcast during prime time in the United States and Canada in May of that year.[60]

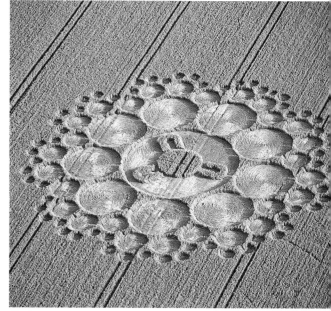

III. 169

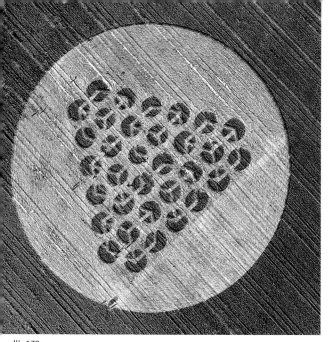

III. 170

What was not shown on the program: In order to create this impressive pattern at night, cranes and floodlights were used. Unfortunately for NBC, the local residents had observed this, in spite of the remote production location, and spread the word. And photos taken from the ground of the forgery quickly disappeared from the Internet: they had shown quite a confusion of bent and broken stalks in the interior of the circle.[61]

The famous trio was at it again in 1999. During the night before July 29 they and four helpers were at work at Avebury for the large English newspaper the *Daily Mail*. In about five hours the hired forgers supposedly created a formation approximately 110 yards (100 m) wide in a wheat field, though

they still owe final proof of the facts. On the next day this produced an amazing three-dimensional effect when looked at from a bird's-eye view (III. 170). But from the ground it looked different: the wheat stalks on the inside of the circle, especially, were in disarray, as though they had been forced down helter-skelter (III. 171). The entire thing look more like "crop damage." The hoaxers had even tried to straighten out the bent stalks again, but without success.

The newspaper's experimental formation, reports of several of the media notwithstanding, already had been disputed before it was uncovered as a "hoax." The fact that *Daily Mail* author Samantha Taylor left this out of her "revelation" story does not make it less true. She presented a whole group of amazed "believers" who were convinced that the Avebury formation was authentic. But she very deliberately ignored other opinions, such as that of German crop circle researcher Andreas Müller.[62] Although Sam Taylor interviewed him for an entire hour, Müller was not given one word in her story—a typical method, used by tabloids even 10 years earlier, of mentioning only things that support their thesis.

The pattern of one-sided stories in the sensational press is quite frequently the following: Journalists pretend to be open and impartial, and dishonestly gain the confidence of those they interview. If these people say things that don't fit into the preconceived story they are simply left out. Statements that fit the notions of the reporter, however, are used as "proof"—

proof, for example, of how naively crop circle investigators act; how they are all victims of a pure swindle. On the other hand, no one who is taken in and fooled by the media in this way, either out of naivety or thoughtless narrow-mindedness, deserves any pity. As boring as the stereotypical cynicism of a newspaper such as the *Daily Mail* may be, one benefit is that it keeps all crop circle researchers who conscientiously keep testing their knowledge on their toes. In the end they'll also encounter journalists who are trying to learn and pass on true knowledge. Stylistically similar to Sam Taylor's *Daily Mail* story was the German Silke Hohmann's September 1999 article in *Journal Frankfurt*, which took up an entire page to dismiss crop circles based on one-sided information presented in one of a series of lectures at an event called "Placebo." Her article, entitled "Is Anybody There?" also pretended competence in a misleading way, using sloppy, trite sayings.

The only really original thing about the event, organized by church groups in Frankfurt, was the fact that Englishman Rod Dickinson was called in as an "expert." Dickinson is one of a group of crop circle forgers known previously as "Team Satan." So this former member of "Team Satan" gave a lecture about crop circle photographs to the assembled Christian congregation.

He didn't mention his own experiences with puzzling appearances of light (see "Signals from Outer Space?" page 112), which he and his "Satan's comrades" repeatedly claimed to have had when creating the fake circles and which he likes to relate at other opportunities. In any case the poor German listeners were no wiser in the end: Dickinson gave his lecture in English, without any translation.

The organizers were not interested in others' opinions either. When Andreas Müller suggested to the organizers that perhaps they should also invite someone from the field of crop circle research to speak, they ignored him.

Other man-made crop circles that were at their most impressive when seen from the air were created in 1999. In a single night a 15-person team made a "perfect" crop circle—as they called it—on the Island Schouwen-Duiveland in the Netherlands. Project "Fe-Male," 220 yards (200 m) in diameter, was the largest artwork in grain created by humans up to that point. Project initiator Remko Delfgaauw, 33 years old, said about this type of landscape art: "Project 'Fe-Male' was a complete success for us. Many people looking at the aerial photos cannot believe that people are capable of creating such a work. That is a compliment and helps me to overcome doubts about the crop circle phenomenon." Delfgaauw sees himself "now more as an nonbeliever." Although he believes in extraterrestrial life, he does not make a connection between crop circles and the extraterrestrial any longer.

"Creating crop circles is habit-forming," says Delfgaauw. "That goes for me and for the friends I work with. We have in no way reached the end of our efforts. We have the competence and the will to complete the largest and most perfect crop circle project that has ever been." This self-confident businessman thinks that a "work of art" such as this could become a reality as a "unique team-building project" involving more than 60 people.[63]

In its entry on the Internet, the "Fe-Male" team assures the reader that it does not intend to "make fun of the authentic phenomenon" through its activities. This makes us curious about what people, on the one hand, and the "authentic phenomenon," on the other hand, will conjure up in the countryside in the future.[64]

It cannot be denied that the Dutch team as well as the British "CircleMakers" understand their craft. The aerial photos are impressive. More to the point would be to see what the details look like from the ground.

The Circles of the Aged

How far back does the story of forgers go? In 1983, the British newspaper the *Daily Express* (not to be confused with the *Daily Mail*) tried to fool its competition in the *Daily Mirror* by having a circle created in the vicinity of Westbury, Wiltshire.[65] But the history of hoaxes goes back even further if Doug Bower is to be believed: "I had always been interested in UFOs and flying saucers," the retiree says. He claims to have created a small circle already in 1978 in a wheat field in Hampshire County "to imitate the imprint of a flying saucer," he says.[66] From then until the 1990s he had help creating circles from his retiree friend David Chorley, who has since died. They became world famous in 1991.

Circle fever had reached its zenith in southern England at the time. Then, on September 9th, the world of crop circle researchers collapsed: "The Men Who Conned the World" was the gigantic headline in the British tabloid *Today*. The paper, owned by the Murdoch concern, "revealed" that "the mysterious crop circles that had puzzled scientists of the entire world" were a "gigantic fraud." Doug Bower, 67 years old then, and David Chorley, 62, were celebrated as the solution to the puzzle. Equipped with ropes and boards, they had created the hoax. But the two sprightly retirees could not verify their adventuresome anecdotes with either photos or other records.

Reporters from all over the world and dozens of television teams were all the more interested in attending a press conference set for September 10th at Chilgrove in Sussex. In front of cameras, Doug and Dave created dumbbell-shaped figures in a field inside of an hour. But neither this first figure nor a second circle created later for the press was convincing, according to the author of the book *Crop Circles*, Michael Hesemann, and he quotes the crop circle researcher Colin Andrews: "There is nothing here which could impress us besides two very sporty gentlemen in their 60s. I think we have been taken in by all the media."[67]

The *Today* story and the intensive media response that followed did not fail in effec-

III. 171

III. 171: "The Cube Triangle": a look inside the formation shows the practiced eye that an authentic "CircleMaker" had not been at work (see also III. 170).

tiveness. Obviously two retirees from Southampton creating a fake in front of running cameras had been enough, in spite of being so lame, to put a lasting damper on broader public discussion. Slogans and simple explanations are more acceptable than the questions that remain open.

The "revelation" story had already had a prelude in 1990. Crop circle researchers under the leadership of Colin Andrews undertook an elaborately planned nighttime watch under the sponsorship of BBC television and Japanese Nippon TV. For "Operation Blackbird," the researchers had 24-hour video cameras, infrared cameras, night viewers, and radar, among other things, at their disposal. The project was to last three weeks starting July 23rd.

But after only two days an enthusiastic Andrews reported on an early morning BBC program that "objects of light" had been captured on the sensitive equipment and a new formation now lay there. Colin Andrews made himself ridiculous in a live report in front of a TV audience. He did not imagine at that early morning hour that he had fallen into the trap of a well-organized swindle. "It was only too obvious that everything had been planned," Michael Hesemann wrote. "Even the red wire the same length of one of the six circles was found. Whoever had made this formation must have had the intention to embarrass the crop circle researchers completely: when a meek Colin Andrews had to admit the same day that he had been victim of a huge fraud, he became the laugh-

ingstock of the nation and one reporter after the other left the 'Blackbird' Watch Station of Bratton Castle in amusement."

Crop circle researcher George Wingfield connects the British army with this fraud. He claims to have heard from "a reliable source in the high ranks of the military" that the Bratton fraud was carried out by an army unit on the orders of the Defence Ministry. Wingfield does not exclude the possible reason that the ministry wanted to bring intense crop circle fever under control and at the same time deactivate "Operation Blackbird," which the military was officially involved in. Prior to this, the press had been making louder and louder demands for an official position on this matter.[68]

In spite of elaborate "cases" reported in front of cameras in 1990 and the big "revelation" stories of 1991, not everyone appeared to be convinced that only a couple of retirees or soldiers were behind the crop circles. A crop circle competition was arranged for those people during the night between July 11th and 12th. The idea came from no less than the biologist and well-known critic of orthodox academia, Rupert Sheldrake. The "Crop Circle Contest" was arranged by the German TV program *PM* together with the British daily *The Guardian* and John Michell's journal, *The Cereologist*. According to the rules of the contest all 12 participating teams had to create the identical formation in a field between 10 P.M. and 4 A.M. The prize: 3,000 pounds sterling.

"Many turned up with garden rollers," documentary film producer John Macnish recalls, "others with homemade aluminum tools, some with dogs, and many with bare hands. But all of them had the same intention: to produce as exact a copy as possible of the pattern given by the organizers." Also present at the contest were the "tormentors of the crop circle scene," as Macnish calls them, Rob Irving, Pam Price, and Jim Schnabel, who, besides Doug and Dave, claim to have made an entire series of formations in the early 1990s in southern England.

Macnish had the job of filming the "forgeries" from a helicopter the next morning before the jury was to decide on a winner: "When we flew around the hill of West Wycombe an unforgettable sight greeted us. In the golden wheat beneath us 12 practically identical pictograms were stretched out along the tractor ruts [tracks]. I had tried to imagine what awaited me but I never would have imagined that the actual formations would be so similar." The winning team was led by Adrian Dexter and had used various tools such as stools and painters' ladders. The American Jim Schnabel, a "one-man team," came in second.

But according to Macnish: "Even Rupert Sheldrake was of the opinion that the standard was indeed very high and some of the entries were convincing. But this in itself was no proof that all circles were made by humans. His opinion was: 'Just because it is possible to forge a 20-pound note does not begin to prove that all 20-pound notes are forgeries.'"[69]

In 1992 John Macnish also observed the retiree team of Doug and Dave during their nighttime activities and got their agreement to test them in his own way. They created a pictogram according to his plan. The documentary film producer conceded that the two "had considerable experience in making crop circles and showed speed and talent only few of the participants in the crop circle contest could compete with." Neither the old men nor the farmer who had been told of the project nor Macnish divulged anything of the plan, in order to test the reactions of those who "discovered" it. Many people were impressed. Lucy Pringle fell for the fraud. Colin Andrews, on the other hand, was very cautious after his bitter experiences in the two previous years and did not want to offer an opinion. Pat Delgado did not even bother to come to the site of the event. Only Jürgen Krönig recognized a forgery in the pictogram created by Doug and Dave.[70]

At the same time it was Krönig who stressed that human capacity shouldn't be underestimated: "Whoever has the strong will to do this can create excellent circles and pictograms in grain."[71] So today the big controversy remains over which formations in the grain are "authentic" and which are "fakes." Researchers' estimates of the percentage of circles that are "authentic" range widely; one expert may say 40 percent, another 90 percent. Some believe only a very small number are genuine. And then there are the skeptics who insist that there is no authentic crop circle phenomenon (Ill. 172).

Interestingly, though, the forgers continue to report puzzling appearances that they are confronted with as they are creating the fake circles. "CircleMaker" Julian Richardson, along with several colleagues, claims to have observed an orange-colored ball of light while making a circle: "We stared perplexed at the football-sized light, which floated about 50 feet (15 m) above the ground without moving. About five seconds later the light began to sink down. After an additional five seconds, perhaps still 33 feet (10 m) above the ground, it faded and finally disappeared....Were we witnesses to a natural phenomenon or had we actually observed the authentic circle makers?" Richardson wonders.[72]

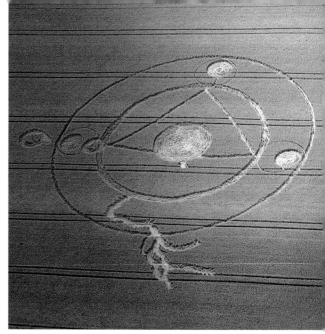

Ill. 172

Ill. 172: There are imitations of this type every year.

The Efforts of Scientists...

Are there "authentic" crop circles in addition to the "fake" ones? Figures whose origin and method of creation cannot be explained? Academics might struggle wth this question, but as a rule they avoid or ignore it. Because in the life view of rationalists, there is no place for whatever cannot be explained (yet). Only what relates to common experience, and the laws built upon that, is accepted. "Following this logic all circles must have been faked right from the start even though there is no proof supporting this opinion," comments the German journalist Jürgen Krönig.[73] Some slightly less orthodox scientists, however, are prepared to do what, in the end, makes any progress in science possible: to take on the subject and look for new explanations.

Among these scientists was Dr. John Graham, director of the agrarian division of the Cranfield Institute of Technology in England. In spite of the revelations already made at the beginning of the 1990s concerning "forgers" such as Doug and Dave, he was certain that the secret of the crop circles had "not been solved." In the American scientific magazine *Science*, John Snow, professor of atmospheric studies at Purdue University, explained that "several circles could be traced back to vortices (whirlwinds)." Japanese scientists in laboratory experiments in Tokyo were able to produce plasma that formed precise circles and rings when an aluminum rod was passed underneath it.[74]

As early as the 1980s meteorologist Dr. Terence Meaden suggested a theory for the appearance of crop circles: that special atmospheric conditions in dry, calm weather led to "plasma vortices," a kind of electrically charged whirlwind, that caused the circles in the fields. But since crop circles appeared even under rainy and windy weather conditions, he later modified his explanatory proposition. From then on he stressed the effect of the vicinity of undulating drafts on the possible formation of downdrafts.[75]

But as more and more complex patterns appeared in the fields at the beginning of the 1990s, Terence Meaden's research proposition was thrown overboard. "It is wrong now to draw certain conclusions from highly uncertain observations," Jürgen Krönig commented. Meaden was also taken in by a group of skeptics in 1991.[76] In spite of this, Meaden's weather thesis, which in the meantime has been superseded entirely, is still cited frequently as *the* explanation for crop circles. (One such case was a documentary program of British television BBC shown on Swiss Channel One at the beginning of December 1999.)[77]

In this connection the leading research engineer at the time at British Aerospace, Thomas Roy Dutton, a participant in air and space travel projects, had already reported in 1991 that plasma vortices followed a mathematical model different from the many crop circle patterns he had analyzed.[78] Based on observations in the field, he came to the conclusion that a simple mathematic model could simulate the circles adequately. So he programmed his computer using this model and made acceptable reproductions of crop circle formations. Upon attempting to transform the resulting pattern into shapes lying in the field, he could not reproduce that form using any of the stimuli known to him. As a result he spoke of a "radiation energy," and we would still need to invent the technology for this.[79]

...And Their Evidence

Dr. William C. Levengood, together with the BLT (Burke, Levengood, Talbott) Research Team, has undertaken the most intensive and complete scientific research into crop circles and accompanying manifestations to date. The American biophysicist has carefully examined grain and soil samples from over 300 crop circles. As far back as 1989 the expert on plant development was called upon to investigate wheat and barley plants taken from two British crop circles. The English crop circle researcher Patrick Delgado sent the plant samples to Levengood's Pinelandia Biophysical Laboratory in Grass Lake, Michigan.

Delgado hoped laboratory analysis would show measurable differences between plants from the crop circles and plants collected in the same grain field but outside of the formations. In fact, Levengood's coworker, Nancy Talbott, recorded the fact that "astonishing anomalies were observed in the structure of the material taken from inside the crop circle."

William Levengood was struck by the purely visual changes in the form and length of the growth nodes, among other things. When he examined the cell structure under the microscope, he also found abnormally enlarged cell wall pits. The cell wall pits are tiny ducts in the semipermeable cell membranes that allow the exchange of matter and fluids. Comparison samples taken from outside the formation in the same field had cell walls without enlarged pits.

Levengood assumed there was a very quick and brief heating of the fluid in the cells: cells swell with lightning-fast increases in temperature. The cell walls and the pits were forced to expand. Cells in experimental plants that the plant physiologist exposed to radiation in a microwave oven demonstrated symptoms similar to the samples from the crop circle when examined under the microscope. But this was only one of many anomalies.

Today Levengood qualifies his work, saying that later scientific experiments found that the enlarged cell wall pits were actually less conclusive and reliable than other anomalies. But the studies have prompted several continuing research projects involving thousands of collected comparison samples.

The BLT Research Team came into existence in 1992. At that time Levengood's findings from the then several dozen crop circles had engendered interest beyond England and the U.S. From this point on, Americans Nancy Talbott and John Burke supported Levengood's work financially and logistically. Thanks to this voluntary help,

BLT could cope with the growing work involved in conducting experiments that were carefully planned, organized, and carried out, and that conformed to all standards of academic science. The psychologist Nancy Talbott is responsible today for field experiments; the physicist John Burke supports the biophysicists in laboratory work.

Since 1994 Levengood, who has published over 50 articles in academic journals such as *Science* and *Nature*, has published three scientific studies with results from his crop circle investigations.

The first study, from 1994, shows the "anatomical anomalies in plants from grain formations."[80] The second, from 1995, discusses a coating of meteoric iron found in a formation in the southern English town of Cherhill. This formation appeared in August 1993 at the time of the Perseid meteor shower. The shimmering covering consisted of particles of iron of meteoric origin melted together. Levengood and coauthor John Burke suppose that this iron oxide dust from meteorites burned in the atmosphere was attracted by magnetic fields associated with the energy of the creation of crop circles. This observation is expected to be examined further in another scientific publication soon.[81] In 1999 Levengood and coauthor Nancy Talbott examined the distribution and flow of energy released by the formation of grain circles.[82] They prove that the anomalies discovered in the plants in question increase linearly the closer they are to the "epicenter" of the formation.

Nancy Talbott summarized the most important plant anomalies that the BLT Team could document:

1. The abnormal enlargement of cell wall pits mentioned above.
2. Extensive enlargement (in both length and thickness) of plant stem nodes (Ill. 173; see also Ill. 161).
3. Clear bending at the growth node of 10 to 90 degrees (sometimes even more), especially on the last and second-to-last node, but also often on all nodes on the stalks (Ill. 174; see also Ills. 64, 87, 161).
4. Growth nodes burst completely open from the inside out, unlike anything found in comparative samples from outside the crop circles (Ill. 175).
5. Stunted, malformed seed heads, with seeds either missing altogether or much smaller than normal in both size and weight.
6. Clear changes in the germination and growth behavior of grain germinated under laboratory conditions from seed taken from crop circles (Ill. 176). The growth rates of the seedlings were measured for 14 days and other characteristics observed. Depending on such variable factors as the age of the plants at the time of creation of a crop circle, the seeds:
   a) Didn't germinate at all.
   b) Germinated, but exhibited clearly diminished growth of the shoots as well as of the roots.

Ill. 173: Enlarged growth nodes burst from inside (see Ill. 161)

Ill. 174: Clear bending and lengthening of the growth nodes (see Ill. 87)

Ill. 175: Burst growth nodes

Above: stalks from a crop circle. Below: stalks from the surrounding field.

Ill: 176: Seeds from plant samples from crop circles often demonstrate clearly worse germination and growth.

Ill. 177: Normal growth in test shoots from outside the formation (All photos Dr. William Levengood)

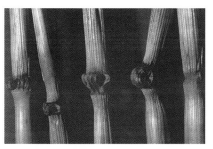

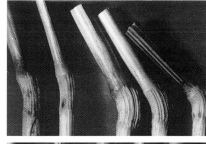

Ill. 173

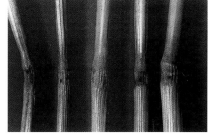

Ill. 174

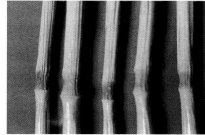

Ill. 175

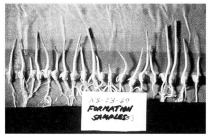

Ill. 176

Ill. 177

c) Germinated, but demonstrated development clearly different from typical growth for the species or variety.
d) Germinated and showed clearly more rapid and stronger development than typical plants.[83]

Talbott stresses that the anomalies listed above are always in comparison to test samples of plants collected from outside the crop circle but in the same field. "Dr. Levengood never knows from which country the samples come to him and which are from inside or outside a crop circle." Only under those circumstances does the scientist compare the data found in the laboratory with the collection records.

The BLT Team finds a combination of the abnormalities listed above in a great majority of the samples studied (in 1999 they came from Canada, the United States, England, the Netherlands, and Israel), "with very high statistical significance," Nancy Talbott stresses. The research group uses the threshold of 95 percent as the valid level of significance, as required in scientific studies. That is, the great majority of the plant samples studied by the BLT team lead to the conclusion that the anomalies occur at least 95 percent of the time.

The greater the number of statistically significant results the researchers can collect, the greater the probability that it means, in effect, deviations from the norm, when taken all together. The probability of an actual anomaly lies on a whole far above 95 percent.

In a 1999 study, William Levengood described precisely his method of collecting plant samples. The sample sizes, he wrote, must be sufficient for statistical analyses. According to a standard plan, groups of 15 to 20 plants are picked from various points within a crop circle.

Each of the collected plant samples is given a simple, distinctive code and the position where the plant was removed is entered exactly on a diagram of the crop circle. The field workers also collect an identical number of plant groups from outside the formation at various distances from the field, but always from the same field, because only the same type plant and seed can be compared. They give these samples codes too and again take careful note of the place from which they are taken. Green, unripened stalks are first dried so that they do not get moldy during their trip to the laboratory.

Levengood's team has been "tested" in many ways already. Assistants always send samples of grain stalks, collected and coded exactly according to the procedure described above, to the Pinelandia Laboratory in Michigan. In one test these samples, unbeknownst to Levengood, came from manmade circles flattened in the field either with boards, rollers, or shoes. In this study, Levengood found that comparison samples from inside and outside of the "artificial" crop circles demonstrated almost no differences. In

several cases, Nancy Talbott adds, certain slight differences in the length of the growth nodes were found, "but having no relation to the other characteristics." After that William Levengood had his own "artificial" crop circles made using boards in an experimental wheat field in Maryland. For each set of four circles, his coworkers flattened two small circles—one or two yards (1 or 2 m) across—in each of two wheat strips grown a yard apart. One strip had been fertilized with nitrogen-rich fertilizer and the other fertilized "normally." The first set of four circles was made on around June 3, the second on June 13, and the third on July 25, 1997, shortly before harvest. The object was to observe the reaction of the stalks to being flattened at various stages of ripeness.

There is a mechanism inherent in the growth nodes of grass and grain stalks that assures that, if flattened horizontally and still green, the stalks will stand upright again. This happens because of the thickening on the underside of the last node on the flattened stalk. This completely natural so-called phototropic or gravitropic reaction takes place after storm damage, for example. The entire stalk above the node is pushed up by means of this thickening. In the area of the node an "angle" or "knee" forms, and the angle increases over time. The natural bending upward in the plants examined by the BLT Team began several hours to three days after being pressed down. In the case of "authentic" crop circles, this clear bending is present immediately when the circle is discovered, often only a short time after it has

come into being. And the bending is from perpendicular to horizontal, contrary to gravitropic behavior (Ill. 64)! It seems probable that this horizontal bending happens very quickly, quite a paradox from a biological point of view.

Comparison studies that involved examining stem nodes under a microscope and precisely measuring them showed that the nodes of flattened wheat stalks collected from inside the test crop circles created by Levengood's fellow workers were around 10 percent longer than those of standing samples from outside the circles. In this case, there was no difference whether the plants came from the overfertilized or normally fertilized strips. Levengood traces this lengthening to the natural gravitropic reaction of the plants.

The lengths of the nodes in samples from crop circles of unknown origin, however, showed changes of between 30 and 200 percent. Such changes, Levengood says, cannot necessarily be explained by natural gravitropic responses, which have little influence on the length of the nodes. Besides that, the plant samples from the mechanically flattened circles showed no further anomalies such as burst growth nodes or changes in the germination or growth behavior of the seeds. Tests with their own crop circles and blind experiments with stalks from other "artificial" formations, which were not known in advance to the BLT team, cause the biophysicist to conclude that the changes listed above in plants could not be caused by a simple mechanical effect, such

III. 178

as flattening of grain by using a roller, boards, or feet.

The plants from authentic crop circles of unknown origin demonstrate "evidence of exposure to rapid air movement, unusual electrical fields, very brief exposure to extreme heat, and ionization in a thermodynamically unstable system," Nancy Talbott explains. "One naturally occurring atmospheric force which includes each of these features," she says, "is a ion-plasma vortex—a very 'high energy' example of which is a lightning discharge."

In 1994 William Levengood presented a ion-plasma vortex theory in a peer-reviewed scientific paper, taking the concept much further than that proposed by meteorologist Terence Meaden. Levengood considered atmospheric ion-plasma vortices the possible causative power behind the formation of crop circles. The field and laboratory data gathered since continue to support this theory, Nancy Talbott believes. "And," she continues, "although it is difficult for most people to imagine, it is entirely possible for such vortices to produce an enormous variety of complex geometrical patterns upon impact at the Earth's surface."

At the same time, however, Talbott stresses that the effect of the "plasma vortex" by no means shows up only in the form of geometric figures: "Sometimes in fields near geometric formations there are patches of flattened grain that lack any comprehensible structure." These types of patches of seemingly randomly flattened grain are not conspicuous compared to the spectacular, precise figures and were often wrongly confused with classical wind damage (III. 178). "Our investigations have shown that the flattened stalks in those types of patches could exhibit the same alterations to plant tissues as those observed in the highly organized geometric patterns," says Talbott. In other cases these "random downed" patches occur by themselves, not in the vicinity of geometric figures.

Along the same lines, the BLT team also has shown that grain formations in countries other than England are usually less perfectly developed and precise as those in England. Particularly in North America, the figures often lack form or display no organized structure. They do display, however, "all the traits" of an authentic formation in detail. Talbott has no explanation for that except possibly the "different weather conditions in North America."

But even Talbott has become careful regarding the southern English crop circles. "Since 1996 we've been taking only a few samples," she says. The risk is too great today of losing too much money and time working with materials from fake English circles. Without questioning the fact that every year in England a great number of authentic formations appear, she warns: "Any attempt to determine a crop circle's origin—whether it's man-made—based entirely on its aesthetic appearance, precision, and complexity, will probably fail."

According to Talbott, the BLT Research team has found the classic anatomical changes in plants described in this section in formations of all types, from "completely disorderly and accidental" to the most elaborate and complex.

William Levengood's plasma vortex theory presents a model of the mechanisms in place during the creation of an authentic crop circle. But Levengood, who carries out his studies in complete seclusion anyway, does not wish to speculate publicly about the possible causes that trigger the "plasma vortex"— whether, for example, a guiding intelligence is behind it.

Even Nancy Talbott is guarded: "Everything is possible!" she laughs. "Using statistical methods we've proven that something that can't be explained is going on. That is already a lot. We're careful with speculations for two reasons: First, we ourselves simply know too little. Second, we've been burned by bad experiences."

The BLT team's studies received unexpected supporting evidence from the Dutchman Eltjo Haselhoff. In his own studies, he took grain and soil samples from two small crop circles that appeared in the night of June 7, 1999, at Hoeven (North Brabant, Netherlands) and tested them. "Growth nodes on the stalks from the formations were sometimes more than double in length," writes Haselhoff.[84] Then, in addition to taking his own objective, independent measurements, he sent samples (which he had collected using Nancy Talbott's method) to Levengood's laboratory in Michigan. Levengood's results: The statistics from samples within the two Dutch circles displayed significant anomalies compared to the samples from outside the circles.

Signals from Outer Space?

Crop circles and the word "extraterrestrial" seem to be inseparably associated with one another. From the start, with the first photographs of circular symbols in Australia and England, the question has been asked: could they be the landing tracks of "flying saucers"? There have been numerous eyewitness accounts of objects of light, small balls of light, or "UFOs" appearing in the night or at twilight—and sometimes during the day—in areas where there are crop circles. Although many of the accounts may seem freely invented, the stories as a whole must be taken seriously. In late summer of 1999, in the Vale of Pewsey in the southern English county of Wiltshire, dozens of people repeatedly witnessed puzzling appearances of light. Some were able to capture them in part on video. In the night before August 5th, a Japanese camera team filmed such lights in this classic crop circle area and even attempted to follow them in vehicles.

The fact that so many people independently of one another have described these lights and have captured them on film—and that we ourselves have witnessed this phenomenon—makes the appearances undeniable. That does not say where the lights come from, even if you call them "UFOs." "UFO" is nothing more than an acronym for "unidentified flying object," which is correct in this usage. But many automatically associate UFOs with extraterrestrial spaceships, or "flying saucers," and consider them more or less obscure and theoretical. The two German authors Joachim Koch and Hans-Jürgen Kyborg see in crop circles "the answer from intelligent beings from Orion." Others consider extraterrestrials from the Pleiades or the star Sirius to be the creators of crop circles.

Even Thomas Roy Dutton, leading research engineer at British Aerospace, considers crop circles a sign of extraterrestrial intelligence—but he is more cautious. After examining computer analyses of dozens of aerial crop circle photos, he reaches the following conclusion in an interview with Michael Hesemann: "It appears as though we are dealing with technology thet is far superior to ours. Therefore we must assume that it is of extraterrestrial origin."[85]

UFOs pop up often in Hesemann's book, *Crop Circles*. But the best-selling German author, historian, and cultural anthropologist is careful about using the term. He stresses: "'UFO' does not necessarily mean 'spaceship.'" He dedicates an entire chapter to the "UFO connection" and quotes in it a long series of witnesses who report UFO sightings in circle territory. For example, he relates the story of Mary Freeman from Marlborough, who was on the way home in her car on the evening of July 13, 1988: "But what was that?" he writes. "An intense, gold-white glow came out of the clouds, descended slowly, silently and majestically—brighter than the full moon. She took a brief look at the road ahead of her, then again at the mysterious shining object. At this moment a

III. 179

thin ray of white light appeared to come from it at an angle of perhaps 65 degrees, and fell on the area in front of Silbury Hill.... On the morning of July 15, 1988, Farmer Robert Hues discovered the first of five 'Celtic crosses' that would appear that summer on his land in the area of Silbury Hill. The cube-shaped pattern 97 yards (88 m) wide lay exactly at the place where Mary Freeman saw the 'thin ray of white light' go down two nights earlier. Coincidence?... Actually, Mary Freeman's experience is only one of a series of incidents that suggest at

least some connection between the crop circles and the UFO phenomenon."[86]

British crop circle researcher Colin Andrews also has compiled various reports that show a connection between crop circles and unidentified lights. The English crop circle photographer Steven Alexander, too, has collected cases of appearances of light related to crop circles and has himself witnessed the phenomenon. In 1990 he filmed a low-flying disc above a field in Alton Barnes, where a large crop circle had just turned up. "The small blinking object dove into the grain field now and then before it

became visible again," says Alexander. When it floated over to a neighboring field, a young farmer also clearly saw it. The farmer reported that his tractor's motor had stalled as the light object crossed his path.[87]

In 1994 the same area at Alton Barnes was the scene of a similar sighting by a group of crop circle researchers searching at night for a newly created formation in East Field (III. 27). A helicopter (perhaps military?) also was involved at this sighting. In 1998 we made a similar observation again, in the same area. As we were going to a seven-sided crop circle in East Field after 11 P.M., a moving helicopter flying extremely low over the field disturbed the nighttime quiet. It was not entirely visible from our observation point, because of a hilltop and distance, but other witnesses described the scene exactly. The helicopter was following a small shining object.

A young Englishman claims to have filmed similar light objects in the early morning of August 11, 1996, from the hill at Oliver's Castle. The eight-second video shows two small shining objects fly twice over a wheat field, circling just above the grain and then disappearing. During those same eight seconds the stalks in the field are flattened and form a snowflake-type formation (III. 67).[88] The video caused a lot of debate. If it was authentic and not, as some people maintained, doctored using a computer, this would be the first time the creation of a crop circle had ever been filmed. Crop circle researcher Andreas Müller from Saarbrücken, who is in charge of the International Crop Circle Archives (ICCA), says concerning this: "New analysis of the video shows that these small balls of light come from a much larger shining object in the background and return to this object afterwards."

American crop circle researcher Ilyes describes a comparable case involving several Czech researchers. In the night between August 7 and 8, 1997, at the foot of Milk Hill near Alton Barnes, the Czechs observed a large bright light from which three successive sets of smaller lights emerged in the star-studded sky and made low passes over the field. The points of light flew directly to the field and after a short time returned to the object from which they came. At the break of day on August 8th, a huge, complex star formation was discovered at the foot of Milk Hill, a high point of the year 1997 (III. 96).

Numerous video documentaries on crop circles include the sequence of the lights filmed at Oliver's Castle. Colin Andrews is right when he says in an interview in one such video: "It is not so important whether this is authentic or fake. In any case it shows concretely how crop circles could arise." He should know. In 1993, on behalf of a United Nations staff subgroup, he interviewed around 70 people who claimed to have witnessed the creation of a crop circle. Based on their statements he was able to determine a variety of details concerning the creation of a circle, such as the time involved and the occurrence of various phenomena such as light and sound.

Because of these documented cases and the controversies that arose around them, several individuals came down from their ivory towers of academic wisdom and commented. For example, in the German magazine *Illustrated Science*, the German science journalist Jan Tuber actually reported the following in 1997 as pioneering news: "Grain fields all over the world in the 1970s and 80s showed strange patterns....And people thought that they came about because of the takeoff or landing of UFOs," he said, repeating well-known suppositions.[89] "All of them turned out to be the work of pranksters," he judged in a sweeping conclusion, most probably without ever having visited a crop circle.

Ironically, the article was dedicated to the astronomer and space researcher Carl Sagan, who had just died in 1996 and was also known for his unorthodox statements. He had stirred up quite a lot of controversy with his statement a few years earlier on the importance of global change to keep the planet habitable: "We may be too foolish to perceive even what the real dangers are, or that much of what we hear about them is determined by those with a vested interest in minimizing fundamental change."

Extremes Collide

Totally independent of crop circles, the notion of extraterrestrial life has become a subject of debate that separates people into two simple groups: believers and nonbelievers. The believers, in turn, are themselves divided into two camps: those who think of extraterrestrials as unfeeling aggressors who would attack the Earth like locusts, much as portrayed in Roland Emmerich's film *Independence Day*, and those who view extraterrestrials as our intelligent friends and helpers from outer space, as in Steven Spielberg's films *Close Encounters of the Third Kind* and *ET*.

The nonbelievers, too, are divided: those who do not believe there is physical life anywhere else at all in the universe, and those who believe there is life beyond Earth in outer space but that it could never visit our planet because of the incomprehensible distances involved.

But the nonbelievers can be confronted with a large amount of factual material difficult to ignore. One of the most spectacular cases occurred in 1991 in Belgium, when the chief of the Belgian air force, General Wilfried de Brouwer, made unmistakably clear in a public report distributed by civil, military, and political offices that the airspace over Belgium had been visited and will continue to be visited again and again by flying bodies. These flying objects escape present physical understanding. Without a doubt a day will come when people will understand this phenomenon.[90]

Major Nick Pope of the British Defense Ministry describes in his book *Open Skies, Closed Minds* a "massive wave of UFO sightings with many police and military witnesses" in southwest England during the night before March 31, 1993. In addition to numerous phone calls from private citizens to local police stations in Devon and Cornwall, reports from many night patrols confirmed unprecedented numbers of sightings of strange appearances of light.[91]

Another spectacular case occurred in the United States, also in the early 1950s. In the summer of 1952, 14 UFOs flew low over no less a location than the White House in Washington, D.C. The armed forces followed the craft on radar and sent a fighter plane into the air in response. Reportedly the unknown craft appeared ungainly and awkward. Air Force General Sanford indicated in

a press conference: "The United States Air Force has investigated approximately 2,000 reports of this kind in the past years. Many can be dismissed with ordinary explanations. But there are some credible reports of incredible events. None of the observations, however, allow us to conclude that the U.S.A. is threatened by this."[92] Unfortunately, this would be the first and last press conference with that sort of openness about UFOs in the United States given by any government office.

Astronauts from various countries also have reported unusual observations or speculated about the existence of extraterrestrial life. American astronaut Gordon Cooper claims to have observed "an entire formation of metallic, shining, lens-shaped flying bodies" in the airspace above Munich in 1951 as a pilot. In another case he claimed to have succeeded in filming the landing of a flying saucer. Of course these photos were later put under lock and key in Washington. Gordon Cooper made these statements on a video transmission on the occasion of a three-day congress on "Dialogue with the Universe" in Düsseldorf, Germany. American astronaut Brian O'Leary reported in his book *Exploring Inner and Outer Space* about experiences with unknown technologies and life forms.[93]

Switzerland's astronaut Claude Nicollier also has spoken affirmatively about the possibility that extraterrestrial life exists, noting that life developed on earth and that the same conditions may exist in outer space. There are good reasons to believe that there

are planets orbiting around other stars besides our sun, he said in an interview with the Swiss weekly newspaper *Die Weltwoche*.[94]

On the Russian side, test pilot Marina Popowitsch, former wife of the well-known cosmonaut Pawel Popowitsch, broke through the wall of silence with her 1991 book *UFO Glasnost*. Upon surveying her fellow pilots, she received over 4,000 descriptions of mysterious objects in the sky, which had been observed from airplanes or located on radar. This test pilot with 50,000 hours of flying experience claims to have been a witness herself to "sensational UFO appearances," as she reported in an address in Lakeland, Florida, in April 1990.

In Switzerland there has been no official stance on the subject to date. In the meantime military documents and radar reports have become available that point to the fact that apparently unexplained sightings and events also have taken place in that country.[95]

"The Return of the Gods"

Waves of sightings by some 10,000 witnesses took place in the 1990s in Mexico. Radar reports of UFOs were followed by numerous discoveries of markings in sugar beet and corn fields. The video *Voyagers of the Sixth Sun* includes interviews with biologists who claim to have discovered in these fields new types of plants unknown to them, which seemingly had grown there overnight.[96] There was a wave of sightings as never before in Mexico at the time of the total eclipse of the sun on July 11, 1991. On that Sunday just after midday, millions of people waited for the event. But before the start of the complete eclipse at 1:30 P.M., which was to last six and one-half minutes, thousands of people saw unknown flying objects in the sky. The objects were supposedly visible for several hours on that day. Waves of observations continued in Mexico over the coming years.

In Atlixco, Mexico, a town of 100,000 inhabitants, 90 percent of the population has sighted UFOs, according to estimates of the local media. Miguel Angel Ordonez Rosales, Atlixco's mayor, was the first Mexican representative who took an official position on UFOs in a press conference. In 1992 he stated in front of the local media: "Neither the military nor the government feels threatened by the unknown visitors. No one knows what they are, but they do exist. Everyone is curious."[97]

At the beginning of 1996 I (Werner Anderhub) was also drawn to Mexico by curiosity. I had the opportunity to visit Carlos Diaz at that time. Diaz is known for his excellent photographs of UFOs. In the vicinity of his town of Tepoztlan, considered one of the holiest of places by the region's Indian population (Ill. 180), appearances of light and UFOs have been observed often (Ill. 181). There are always "landings" involved, according to Diaz and other natives. Various people in the streets of the small nearby town of Morelos confirmed such observations for me.

During my stay in Mexico, there were sightings across the entire country of sometimes whole squadrons of unknown flying bodies. I was with Carlos Diaz on the evening of January 28th towards 8:20 P.M. to observe the night sky out in the open. Because of a mountain chain that cut off our view, we weren't able to observe one of the many low flights of objects of lights observed in Mexico that night, which we would reconstruct later. The next day, a day of travel, several people described the event to us.

"You should have been here yesterday evening about 8:30," one Indio exclaimed, greeting my brother and me with shining eyes as we reached the Paso del Cortes in the vicinity of Popocatepetl, a volcano 17,991 feet (5,452 m) high. Several hours before our arrival, a gigantic object of light had come from the direction of Mexico City and flown toward the large volcano, causing great excitement among the local population. The Indio, still visibly excited, told us the light had floated above the high, 12,000-foot (3,600 m) Cortez Pass (Ill. 182) for half an hour before it shot upward and disappeared.

Is It Actually Human Technology?

Could it be humans—but not those who go into the fields at night with rollers or boards—who are making the most complex and puzzling crop circles?

Ill. 180

Again and again human satellite technology is mentioned in discussions concerning the possible origin of crop circles. The notion that laser beams, for example, guided via satellites, could be directed onto the earth's surface like a drawing tool need not be considered completely groundless.

The fantastic precision of laser beams is well known; lasers have become a part of everyday life. Laser beams read information from CDs in the computer on which this text was written. They're a dependable, indispensable aid in surgery. The list of examples of

III. 181

their uses is virtually endless. The possible uses of laser technology for both civil and military applications are unlimited. A person who believes that secret military research in radiation technology could someday produce unpleasant results can hardly be dismissed as a "conspiracy theorist." On the contrary, some say, any other supposition would be naive, considering the continuing horrendous expenditures worldwide for military research and the state-sanctioned secrecy surrounding that research, even in democracies.

Roy Dutton, the British research engineer introduced earlier in this book, is among those who think a laser type of energy beamed down from a great height to the earth may be responsible for the formations.

He points out, however, that humans haven't developed such a technology, one that can flatten plants in precise patterns without destroying them.[98] He's probably right. But perhaps he underestimates the fruits of secret military research.

It is no longer news that world powers have moved their war games into space, into the earth's orbit. Former U.S. president Ronald Reagan left no doubt of this in his time in office in the 1980s. The military satellite project, SDI (Strategic Defense Initiative) was one of his favorite expensive toys. In a historic speech on March 23, 1984, he came out strongly for building this "protective shield" in outer space. It was to consist of space stations equipped with laser weapons programmed to locate and destroy enemy rockets—and, perhaps, for some other purpose.

Following the November 19 to 20, 1985, summit meeting in Geneva between Reagan and the former Soviet Union's newly elected chief, Mikhail Gorbachev, Reagan reportedly said of one part of their discussions: "Just think how easy his task and mine might be in these meetings that we held if suddenly there was a threat to this world from some other species from another planet outside in the universe. We'd forget all the little local differences that we have between our countries and we would find out once and for all that we are all human beings here on this earth together." Apparently the purely earthly threats to the environment were not enough. How else could the tremendous costs for these sorts of "defense" games be

III. 180: The holy mountains and pyramids around Tepoztlan, location of many attested UFO sightings. Natives speak of "El Luz."

III. 181: For years Carlos Diaz has photographed and made videos of impressive objects of light, which appear to be organic rather than of a technological nature. (Photo Carlos Diaz)

III. 182: View from the peak of 17,991-foot-high (5,452 m) Popocatepetl above the Cortez Pass toward the volcano Iztaquatl. According to various witnesses we had just missed a UFO sighting by a few hours.

III. 182

justified, even at the end of the cold war? This is apart from the fact that there are hints the American government felt threatened and still does by "EBEs" (Extraterrestrial Biological Entities).[99]

In any case, the idea that crop circles are the result of satellite-directed radiation experiments makes little sense in the end—if only for the reason that military people are hardly likely to create such delicate and complex works of art. Even Nick Pope finds it unreasonable to accept laser weapons as the possible explanation for the crop circles.[100] Pope was asked by the British Defense Ministry at the end of the 1980s to handle questions from concerned or curious people who were contacting the ministry in increasing numbers about crop circles and other phenomena. So Nick Pope was in a position to bring together a large number of exciting documents on this subject, which were finally used as the basis for his book *Open Skies, Closed Minds*.

The British Defense Ministry first became involved with crop circles in 1985. When a farmer found a "quintuplet" on his land, he informed the local air force base in Middle Wallop, in Hampshire County in southern England. He believed there was a a connection between air force helicopters and what lay in his field. Lieutenant Colonel Edgecombe, who investigated the case, disputed the idea that something like that could be caused by a hovering helicopter's rotor blades. He thought that the military had nothing to do with the matter at all.[101]

Ill. 183

That didn't stop Marc Roberts, the author of the 1995 book *The New Lexicon of the Esoteric*, from writing the following 10 years after the case: "In the meantime it is certain that crop circles were made with the help of helicopters."

A Bed in the Field for Mating Hedgehogs?

Meanwhile, rotating helicopter blades are not the only strange and persistent explanations proposed for the creation of crop circles (Ill. 183). At the time of the simple circle motifs in the 1980s, it was not uncommon to hear suggestions that animals had created the "nests" in the fields. Such opinions were expressed again and again by farmers, hunters, and biologists. And they were meant very seriously. But if anyone nowadays insists on the idea that crop circles are

actually the sleeping places of wild animals such as deer, rabbits, or foxes, they're either going around in circles themselves or are simply joking (Ill. 184). Naturally there is no limit to such fantasy: hedgehogs who run around in a circle in a mating ritual?

From time to time the farmers themselves come under suspicion. So the question could be posed: "Is it possible that the farmers deliberately spread a certain kind of fertilizer that after a period of time causes the grain to fall over? Or that they mow in certain patterns?" To put it mildly this idea, often suggested in connection with the supposition that farmers can make money from crop circle visitors, is met with little understanding among the farmers themselves.

Another suggestion that comes up repeatedly is that the photos of crop circles could simply be retouched photomontages. The notion is certainly not unfounded—good

HERZSCHRITTMACHER

Ill. 184

photomontages can be made of any subject these days.

But the readers of this book can be certain that none of the photos here are montages. Anyone who needs to be convinced with his or her own eyes should look at the travel tips in the appendix of this book.

The Power of Thoughts

Ill. 183: The rotor blades of low-flying helicopters are repeatedly put forward as the explanation for circles.

Ill. 184: According to some, the mating rituals of wild animals are the origin of crop circles.

There are still other possibilities as to how humans could be considered the originators of crop circles: for instance, by the influence of the power of conscious and unconscious thought. Crop circle researcher and author Andy Thomas discusses this possibility at length. He describes the supposition that the power of the collective subconscious could project human thought complexes into the fields and then create and direct plasma vortices. According to Thomas, the geometrical figures that arise this way could correspond to symbols from the collective unconscious, as the Swiss Carl Gustav Jung has described them: symbols as "keys which are activated by the power of the unconscious....Their meaning is independent of the control of consciousness."[102]

The French philosopher and educator of Bulgarian descent, Omraan Mikhaël Aïvanhov, wrote of the geometrical figures that their language was a "language par excellence": "The geometrical figures are like a structure; they are like the scaffolding of reality. These forms which are reduced to bare skeletons are not lifeless on account of this, because they make visible the realities which are in humans and the universe."[103]

Also, professor of anthroposophy K. H. Türk assumes that the pictograms are a reflection of the condition of our soul, and its evolution goes along with the level of change in consciousness on earth. "So the people on earth are themselves the creators of crop circles through the stance of their consciousness."[104]

In connection with the fields of influence produced by the power of thoughts, Rupert Sheldrake's model for explaining the origin of the forms also is mentioned repeatedly. The well-known professor of biochemistry and cell biology writes that the integrity and self-organizing character of systems, no matter how simple or complex they may be, can be traced to the influence of "morphic or morphogenetic fields" that act like "invisible blueprints": "They have a type of inbuilt memory. This memory depends on the process of morphic resonance, the influence of like upon like through space and time....The fields play a formative role in an analogous way to architectural plans."[105]

The enormous creative and formative power of human thoughts, be they conscious or unconscious, involved directly or indirectly or not at all in the creation of crop circles, cannot be underestimated. "Thought is fluid form—and form is fluid thought," the German-trained psychologist and best-selling author Thorwald Dethlefsen said in a lecture in Munich in May 1996. In other words, every material form created by humans has its origin in thoughts, in ideas. Every form, be it a house, a set of dishes, or a car, must be devised or "discovered"—each according to a concept. Only after that is it compressed, stored on paper or electronically on computer, and turned step by step into concrete, comprehensible, "material" form.

Franz Bardon, in his step-by-step, 10-stage instruction book, *The Path of the True Adept*, allows no question unanswered concerning the creative power humans can unleash by learning to control and consciously direct their thoughts. According to Bardon (who himself has already reached the third stage, an accomplishment that most certainly requires much patience, fortitude, and discipline) "occult abilities" appear without their actually being the primary

III. 185

object of the exercises Bardon describes. Even more, he says, the abilities appear as "natural side effects."[106] Without going into too much detail, there are numerous well-documented examples of people with such "supernatural" abilities as—to name a few—telepathy (transference of thoughts), "tumo" (producing warmth, especially well known in ancient Tibet), levitation (overcoming gravity), and telekinesis (moving objects by means of the power of thought). Why shouldn't it also be possible, by means of conscious, concentrated thought power, to project crop circle figures onto a grainfield?

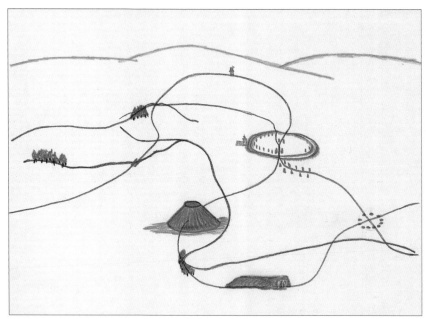

III. 186

III. 185: Stonehenge: Astronomy professor Gerald Hawkins considers this site a prehistoric astronomical computer. The fact that the builders knew much about the structure of our solar system is evident in the way the stones are arranged to mark the beginnings of the seasons.

III. 186: Energy lines join the locations of prehistoric buildings and sites. Where did earlier cultures get their knowledge of these arteries of life? What was the purpose of their layout? (Drawing Miller/Broadhurst)

III. 187: This fractal circle from 1998 at Silbury Hill was one of many crop circles that have appeared in the vicinity of prehistoric buildings and sites.

Gaia—Mother Earth as a Living Being

"There is not only purely physical environmental pollution from well-known causes such as exhaust, waste water, chemicals, poisonous waste, radioactivity, etc., but there is also a type of 'soul waste.' And if we determine today that, for example, the earth and atmosphere are rebelling with earthquakes, tornadoes, climate changes, and so on, why shouldn't the 'soul of the world' rebel too and cause phenomena which could wake us up to our actions?"[107] Thus the anthroposivist K.H. Türk proposes a further approach, the Gaia theory.

The Gaia view is held by many primitive peoples, but also by many in modern society. They speak of Mother Earth and consider the earth to be a conscious, living organism, comparable in many ways to the human body. Earth's life force and development are considered analogous to the body's vitality and development, which are dependent upon a system of intact "life arteries"—such as nerves and blood vessels—as well as delicate energy lines, or "meridians." The Gaia thesis holds that our home planet also is covered with life arteries and energy lines. Locations with special radiation power and energy lie where these meridians intersect or connect (Ill. 186). From time immemorial cultures have made use of this knowledge worldwide. Even today there are frequently holy structures or cult sites, such as stone markers, earthen walls, and even pyramids, at those types of special places of power. At Stonehenge, Europe's most famous cult site, 12 such energy lines are said to converge (Ill. 185). Frequently Christians erected their churches and cathedrals at these locations as well, whether to take possession of the old "heathen" places or—as was the case with many Gothic cathedrals—with the knowledge of the sacred power of such places. In areas of England and France it is easy to find these places, since they were mostly marked clearly with stones. The knowledge of these delicate power fields and energy lines and their connection to one another is called "geomancy."

In this connection it is obvious that many of the crop circle signs have appeared in the immediate vicinity of prehistoric structures and sites (Ill. 187; see also Ills. 2, 3, 35, 56, 72, 80, 84, 100, 117, 142, 147, 187). Could it actually be the earth itself that communicates to us with these symbols? Crop circle researcher Colin Andrews got a hint in this direction from the North American Hopi Indians. Andrews related at a lecture in England in 1995 that when he showed the Hopi photos of crop circles from Wiltshire, they said they were especially shaken by a formation of August 1, 1990 (Ill. 188): "Mother Earth Cries." On August 1, 1990, the second Gulf War, one of the most cynical wars of the last century, began with the invasion of Iraqi troops into Kuwait.

Signs from the Inner World?

Much less commonly than extraterrestrials, "innerterrestrials" are sometimes connected with the origin of crop circles on Earth's surface. Disciples of this concept proceed from the idea that the earth is hollow and that inside of the planet a highly developed race of people lives. They cite a controversial "missing diary," purportedly written by American Navy Admiral Richard Evelyn Byrd, in which he claims to have reached the inside of the earth on a flight over the North Pole on February 19, 1947. There the inhabitants of the inner earth gave him a "message for the people of the outer world." Byrd is said to have described the fantastic achievements of this culture in the "diary," including how the inhabitants of the inner earth used shining "saucer-shaped flying discs" for transportation. The inner earth dwellers had tried again and again, the account goes, to establish contact with the people of the earth's surface by way of those flying discs, in order to warn them about the reckless use of dangerous technologies. "But all our attempts were answered with aggressiveness. Our flying discs were pursued by your military airplanes and shot at," the chief of the inner world told him, according to the book. From there the diary's story continues, with the admiral claiming to have gotten the order to bring a message of warning to the people of the outer earth. "I was placed under the strict surveillance of the National Security Agency of the USA," the author writes in the book, after he had reported at a meeting at the Pentagon on March 1, 1947, about his

experiences. "I received the command to keep silent—for the benefit of mankind. Unbelievable! And I was reminded that I was an officer and therefore must obey their command."

If the story is true, Byrd, who had become world famous through a spectacular flight over the Atlantic in June 1927, placed the orders of the American military above the importance of the message from inner Earth. It may be that he only covered up a freely invented fantasy, which incidentally he is said to have claimed took place a second time in 1957, this time into the inner world through an opening at the South Pole.[108]

That the earth might be hollow contradicts every current teaching about the structure of the planet—upon which, incidentally, a whole series of seismic and other physical laws of nature are built. But up till now no one has bored deeper into the earth's crust than around six miles (10 km). And as long as that remains the case, we can only assume and extrapolate the qualities inside of the earth. The picture handed down by science of Earth's structure remains for the present a functioning but, in the end, unproved model. And individual voices that say that the discs and balls of light that have been observed worldwide came from the inner earth and imparted their messages about the symbolism of crop circles will not remain silent.

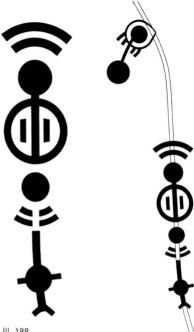

Ill. 188

Ill. 188: This pattern, from a crop circle of August 1, 1990, caused the Hopis to express a concern: "Mother Earth cries." In Hopi symbolism the earth here is hit by an arrow. (Diagram Wolfgang Schindler)

IV The Universal
Language

Geometry—
Symbols of Creation

Symbols are the highest effective powers of nature, which are enclosed in the simplest possible form.

—*Mária Szepes*

Regardless of the origin of crop circles, their fascination, their hypnotic effect, comes from their geometry. What is it that exerts this magical effect and attraction, even in the simplest geometric forms? It is their order, their simplicity, their reduction to the essential. Geometry is *the* language of symbols.

"The only language which can be converted visually and which allows us to enter into contact with an unknown culture or life form is the language of mathematics or geometry. This symbolic language is universal and more easily 'readable' than any other type of writing." Of that Richard Hoagland is convinced. Together with a team of NASA experts, he developed the first interstellar message from mankind: a gold plaque on which are engraved, among other things, geometric symbols; the structure of our solar system; human figures; and mathematical, physical, and chemical formulas. This message has been on its way since the 1970s aboard the Pioneer 10 space probe, which has now left our solar system.[109]

Galileo Galilei, whose proposal that the earth is round shook the crusty clerical structures of the Western world, said: "You cannot understand the universe without learning first to understand the language in which it is written. It is written in the language of mathematics, and its letters are triangles, circles, and other geometric forms. Without this language humans cannot understand a single word of the universe. Without it we wander in a dark labyrinth."[110]

Crop circles are also—with a few noteworthy exceptions—always built on basic geometric elements such as circles, triangles, and squares. In view of our limited knowledge and the number, variety, and increasing complexity of crop circle patterns, it would be presumptuous to try to interpret whole individual formations within the limits of this book. So we will keep to a discussion of a few of the basic geometric building blocks that can transmit "cosmic principles" symbolically.

The book *The Symbolic Language of Geometrical Figures* by Omraam Mikhaël Aïvanhov contains explanations of these basic geometric elements. A philosopher and educator, Aïvanhov was born in Bulgaria in 1900 and lived in France from 1937 until his death in 1986. He was always excellent at explaining to people the complex subjects about which he spoke. Regarding geometric figures, he said that their language was "language par excellence....In order to be able to

interpret these forms, we must enliven them, let the spirit flow into them. As long as we are satisfied to investigate them only externally, they will remain without meaning for us."[111]

The following interpretations of the basic geometric figures are for the most part from *The Symbolic Language of Geometrical Figures*. For a deeper discussion refer to the book itself and to other works on the subject of sacred geometry.

The Circle: "You have surely thrown a stone into water at some time and observed how waves arise from the point of entry into the water and move away in concentric circles. (Ill. 189)....Whoever understands how to decipher the big book of nature cannot fail to recognize a grandiose process in these concentric movements from the center point: The entire creation of the world—everything is revealed in a geometric form.

"The circle, with the point as its center, is allocated an extensive knowledge, a deep philosophy. The circle is the symbol of the universe; the point itself represents the highest being which supports and enlivens the cosmos. Observe once the center point: it is equidistant from all points on the periphery. That way the equilibrium of the circle is preserved. Between the center and the periphery a constant exchange takes place. Through this exchange the life of the entire surface of the circle is created. All life is present there: it vibrates, pulsates, digests, eliminates, breathes, thinks...."[112] The circle, this most perfect of all geometric forms and the basic element of practically all "crop circles," is the symbol of perfect creation. It

symbolizes the highest goal to which we humans can aspire.

The Triangle: "The triangle is actually the fusion of the male and female principles, out of which a third principle arises. In the family these principles are illustrated by the father, the mother, and the child; in chemistry by acids, bases, and salts; in humans by the intellect, the heart, and the will (or thoughts, feelings, and actions); among divine virtues by wisdom, love, and truth (Ill. 190). As the child is the product of the father and the mother, so is salt the product of acid and a base, action the product of thought and feeling, truth of love and wisdom....The equal-sided triangle singly and alone transmits the idea of complete harmony, because it reveals agreement, balance among the three principles" (see Ill. 129).[113]

The Hexagram: (six-pointed star): "This figure, also known as Solomon's Seal or as a symbol of Judaism, consists of two equal-sided triangles, which partially cover and cross over one another. The triangle with the point facing downward illustrates the masculine principle, the triangle with the point facing upwards the feminine....Their union is symbolically represented by the two triangles....The Solomon's Seal is the symbol of those people who have succeeded in developing and strengthening the two principles in themselves, the masculine and feminine, the emissive and receptive. They possess power and gentleness at the same time; they are androgynous, they are perfect."[114] (Ill. 191; see also Ills. 80, 81, 84, 94, 95, 96)

Ill. 189: Circle with ring(s): every event spreads out in waves in the universe (Diagram Andreas Müller)

Ill. 190: The equal-sided triangle: symbol of trinity. With humans, represents man, woman, child (Diagram Andreas Müller)

Ill. 191: The six-pointed star: symbol of the harmonious play between the polarities (Diagram Andreas Müller)

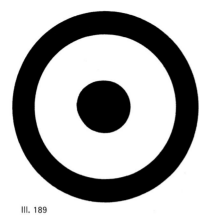

III. 189

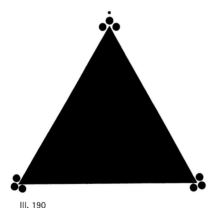

III. 190

III. 191

The Pentagram: "The five-pointed star is the symbol of the complete human (III. 194: see also Ills. 48, 79,105,123). Schematically, the pentagram represents a person who stands on both feet with arms spread out. This position is the symbol of being allied with 'earth and sky'. The feet create the connection with the planet. The hands and the top of the head, on the other hand, are the connection to the 'cosmic consciousness'. In order to achieve this connection, people of various cultures meditate at the beginning and end of the day standing in the position of the pentagram. In nature the trees illustrate the same thing to us. They are connected to the earth by their root system. With their branches they stretch out towards the power of the sun, moon, and stars, connecting with the energy of the cosmos.

"If one studies the name of God in Hebrew, one notices that it consists of four letters: Jod He Vau He. That is the tetragram....The four letters...correspond...to four principles, which dwell in humans: Jod the spirit, He the soul, Vau the intellect, and the second He, the heart. These four principles must manifest themselves, become real by means of a fifth, the will.... Our task now is to live this teaching of the perfect human, thanks to the possibilities which have been given to us, such as the five senses (again the number five): seeing, hearing, smelling, tasting, and feeling. Among them feeling (the sense of touch) is the only sense which is so close to material. Its main organ is the hand with its five fingers....Now we can establish a connection with the five elements again. What are these five elements? Earth, water, air, fire and ether."

The fifth element, ether, is also known as "quinta essentia," as "quintessence" (III. 192; see also III. 76). Although one cannot perceive it with the five given senses, ether is a central element with a higher meaning. This delicate element stands above the four material elements and is a kind of mediator between the physical and the higher dimensions, or stated more simply, a link between the "material world" and the "spiritual world." "Ether" is a very common concept in the realm of transmission technology. If broadcast stations "send tones or pictures into the ether," ether becomes the carrier or transmitter of the vibrations.

"Through their will, their intellect, their heart, their soul, and their spirit, humans are in contact with the five effective elements in the cosmos. For that reason they are in a position to interact with them harmoniously."[115]

The Cross: "It illustrates the masculine principle (vertical beam) and the feminine principle (horizontal beam), which connect in order to be effective together in the universe (III. 193). This cooperation proceeds, however, from a center point, the intersection of the two beams. This center point unifies and hold the powers together. Without this point everything would come apart on the surface as soon as the cross began to turn on its own axis.

"For the cross turns. In this motion around the axis its beams describe a circle, the symbol of the sun. The cross, as it revolves, forms the swastika. This motion

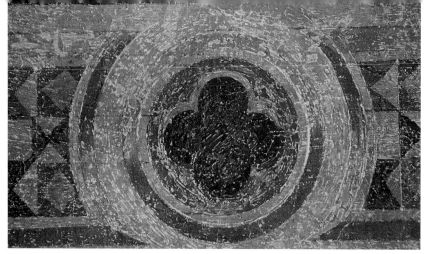

III. 192

III. 193

can go to the right or to the left....A cross rotating to the right illustrates a screwing motion: you secure....the energies in order to control them....If the swastika is turned in the reverse direction, then what was screwed together comes apart, which means the release of physical and instinctive powers. From that follows the immediate exclusion of higher powers of the spirit: you are subject to the mechanical, earthbound side. You can become powerful, but only at the material level....

"The cross is also the representation of the movement of water and fire. At the same time it symbolizes the four directions in space and the four directions of the wind: north, south, east, west. It allows for establishing something further: the constellations of the zodiac form, four at a time, their axes forming three crosses. They are the axes Aries-Libra and Cancer-Capricorn, Leo-Aquarius and Scorpio-Taurus, Sagittarius-Gemini and Pisces-Virgo. In each of the crosses the four elements come up again....

The cross represents also the four currents which traverse the universe, from north to south and from south to north, from east to west and from west to east. In addition to these four streams come two others, which run from zenith to nadir and the reverse. Humans, who stand at the crossing of these streams, are influenced by them and thus should learn to work together with them."[116]

The Squaring of the Circle: "Since time immemorial geometers have tried...to draw a square with exactly the same area as a given circle. They never reached a solution.... They should know, however, that the initiates solved that problem a long time ago. By the example of the trees passing through the seasons of the year, they saw how the bare branches of trees are periodically clothed with leaves, flowers, and fruit. The spirit appears regularly and performs a certain task. This is the circle, therefore the symbol of the limitless, infinite universe. In this circle the square, the material, can with every return of the spirit blossom again and bear

fruit. When the tree enlivened by the spirit bears its fruits, it has solved the problem of the squaring of the circle. A point in time always comes, then, in which the square and the circle agree.... The physical side is tough, but the spiritual side is also hardy. Proof of that: if you destroy the physical body, the subtle bodies live on.... If you destroy a building (the square), the circle continues on indestructible. Wherever it may be, the circle is impossible to destroy, because we are enclosed inside it. It is the cosmic ocean in which we live and breathe."[117]

The Connection to Holy Geometry

In educational institutions geometry is, unfortunately, frequently taught as an abstract, one-sided, rational subject, and for that reason we lose the deeper meaning that dwells inside it. Yet as the examples illustrate, there is more to geometry than angles and linear measure. Since many of the forms

III. 192: "Quinta Essentia": the fifth element, ether, holds the four material elements—fire, water, air, and earth—together. (Mural in the church at Stuls, Graubünden, Switzerland)

III. 193: "Celtic Cross" inside the "Quinta Essentia": axes of the same size indicate the balance of the masculine (vertical beam) and feminine (horizontal beam).

III.194: The Five-pointed Star (Pentagram): symbol of the perfect person (Diagram Andreas Müller)

III. 195: "Square in Circle": symbol of material (square) imbued with the spiritual (circle)

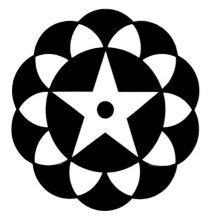

III. 194

appear in crop circles, it may be a matter of concern to their creators that we come to terms with this.

The Square in the Circle (Ills. 195, 145): The square, based on the number four, represents the material on the earthly plane. Everything that is manifested on the planet in material form, the four basic elements, is enclosed by this geometric principle.

If the material (square) is separated from the spirit of the divine (circle), then it is lifeless. The power of the spirit is lacking. Is not overcoming the separation of material and spirit, which has been anchored in the thought patterns of the modern world, one of the most pressing problems of our time? It is especially common these days that the four elements of fire, water, air, and earth are eating away, to an increasing degree, the false, stubborn "order" that has been forced on nature. In 1999 numerous crop circles with fractal geometric patterns based on the number four turned up (see Ills. 138, 148, 150). Do they symbolize the undermining of an old order and the bringing together of a new order—an order in which material is again joined with the spirit?

The Lemniscate (flattened figure eight or infinity sign; Ills. 196, 32): In mathematics this symbol is used to represent unlimited quantity. This means, in other words, neither beginning nor end, or the dissolution of space and time. If the universe is without end, then human life is also a part of this eternity. There is a continuing interchange between the "this side" (the earthly, physical plane) and the "other side" (the metaphysical plane). The concepts of "birth" and "death" are at the same point in the infinity symbol: the intersection of the two circles. Looked at in this way, every dying is at the same time a birth and vice versa. The central point symbolizes the transition from one form of being into the other. It is the alchemist's crucible of "Solve et Coagula," of "dissolving and binding." The Swiss researcher and artist Emma Kunz (see the following section) summarizes this realization in a single sentence: "The number eight mediates between the square and the circle, that is, between earth and heaven."

III. 195

The Spiral: can be seen as the symbol of the dynamic source of power to which the universe, therefore everything, is subordinate (Ill. 197; see also 56, 57, 65). Natural scientists are just beginning to reach a better understanding of this as they look into fractal geometry, to which the spiral form belongs. The mathematician Benoit Mandelbrot developed this branch of science in 1975 and at the same time made possible the access to a "new dimension" with it: researching the interplay of "chaos and order" as a part of nature.[118] If humans learn to understand and accept this, they can participate in an inner and outer process of change in a more relaxed and constructive way. The polarity principle of chaos and order is a direct connection to a transforming movement, the spiral-like circling and fluctuating vibration from one ordering to the next. Like the creation symbol (see below), spirals are found at every level of scale: from the spiral-shaped galaxy to the shell of a snail (Ill. 198) to the DNA chain.[119] As it is above, so it is beneath.

The Creation Symbol or "Vesica Pisces" (Ill. 199; see also Ills. 63, 103, 104): appears again and again in crop circle motifs. At the time of Gothic art this symbol was often immortalized in stone, wood, or glass. Two equal-size circles overlap to their center points, forming a lens-shaped area. This shared area symbolizes the fusion of the feminine and masculine power, which produces new life. This generating and creative act takes place at every point in time on a small and large scale. The first division of a fertilized female egg cell has exactly the form of this geometric symbol.

The Aztec disciple Tlakaelel (see also page 137) sees this creator principle integrated again and again in prehistoric sites. All ancient cultures, whether native to Europe, America, Oceania, Africa, or elsewhere, had some form of so-called sun religion. They were aware of the creative power of the masculine (sun) and feminine (earth). At monuments such as Stonehenge, an astronomical computer and sun calendar of its time, the energetic fusion of cosmic and planetary energy would take place. The unending multiplicity of all life on this planet would be the wonderful expression of the fusion.

This regeneration symbol is manifested even on the cosmic plane. The explosion of a supernova occurs in such form, like a flaming air bubble.[120] "Can new planets arise from the remains of a supernova explosion?" the well-known astronomer Carl Sagan pondered.

Closely connected to the creation symbol is the "Flower of Life" or "Seed of Life" (Ills. 200, 34).

Geometry is the response language of earth, spirit, and heart, and has been considered holy since ancient times.[121] Many highly developed cultures have left geometry's legacy for us in buildings and other depictions. Crop circles may give us new impetus to help us remember again geometry's deeper meaning.

III. 196

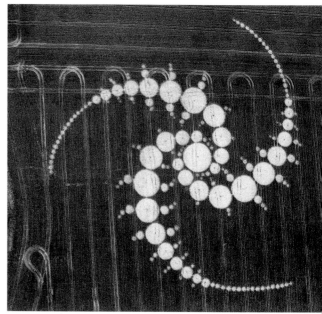

III. 197

III. 198

III. 200

III. 196: "Flat Figure Eight," symbol of infinity

III. 197: "Spirals": symbols of ever-present change

III. 198: Spiral-shaped structure of a snail shell: fractal geometry is a basic element of nature.

III. 199: "Creation," symbol of emergent life in the universe

III. 200: "The Seed of Life": not only immortalized in Gothic architecture but also to be admired in an oat field on the "Stone Avenue" at Avebury

III. 199

129

Emma Kunz—Artwork for the 21st Century

The world is a prelude in our spiritual life. Try to weave the brightest sound into the tone picture.

—*Emma Kunz*

What does the work of Emma Kunz have in common with crop circles? The language of geometry. These common traits seem to us so crucial that we have devoted an entire section to Emma Kunz and the often complex geometric depictions that the Swiss researcher and healer left to posterity. At first glance the geometry of crop circles and Emma Kunz's visual works have little similarity, but the meanings hidden within them may have more in common than you would assume. John Michell, the well-known English geomancer and editor of *The Cereologist*, a journal for crop circle studies, speaks of "revelation" when he thinks of the geometric language of crop circles: "The history of mankind shows us that the revelation was the origin of all cultures and has inspired subsequent renewals. Supposedly it comes at a time in which we need it urgently. Its content is always the same, namely a cosmic law, a canon or collected work of numeric, musical and geometrical harmonies, which is the basis of the predominant order in every civilization." [122]

Michell's statement suggests a connection to the work of Emma Kunz (Ill. 201). The geometric drawings or "energy fields" that

Ill. 201

the Swiss researcher and seer captured with pencil, felt pen, or crayon in large format on graph paper document her knowledge in code. In accordance with her wish, not a single word of her oral explanations was ever written down, although Emma Kunz explained her pictures in great detail. "My artwork is intended for the 21st century," the

artist said. "The time will come when people will be able to understand my pictures."

Emma Kunz was born in Brittnau in the Aargau region of Switzerland. She grew up in the family of a hand-loom weaver. Even as a child she demonstrated a gift for heightened perception. She devoted herself to exploring questions of life and spiritual

Ill. 201: Emma Kunz (1892-1963): The value of her epochal work is gradually being recognized.

Ill. 202: Marigold experiment: after application of magnetic force nine subsidiary blooms grew from one mother blossom—not explicable in plant physiology.

III. 202

connections. Her deep knowledge of energy-related and spiritual powers enabled her to heal people. She also discovered the healing mineral "Aion A" in the ancient Roman quarry in Würenlos in the Aargau region. Today the Emma Kunz Center stands there, and her pictures are exhibited there.[123]

Emma Kunz was able to use her "super-natural" abilities, that is, as seen from the limited vision of the academic world, to influence and change nature. She also repeatedly proved this. For example, she conducted an experiment with several of her friends in her medicinal plant garden that produced sensational results for science. First she showed observers a model of what she intended to do: she had attached five daughter blooms onto the calyx of a marigold with copper wire. Then she walked along the front row of her flower bed with her divining pendulum, letting it swing at the flower plants one by one. Moving from left to right, she gave each plant an "order" loudly and clearly: the first flower was to produce five daughter blossoms, the second seven, the third nine, the fourth eleven, and the fifth thirteen. Without speaking she continued to swing the pendulum over row after row of flowers.

Within days, her friends testified, the number of daughter blooms planned by Emma Kunz had sprouted forth from the calyx of each mother blossom. Astonished, they stood before the row of flowers with five, seven, nine (III. 202), eleven, and thirteen smaller blooms (III. 203). Emma Kunz explained that with this experiment, which in the opinion of academic biology is totally incomprehensible, she had made visible a natural law. Such laws, she said, were extremely simple and entirely obvious. Indeed, they were too simple for our bogged-down intellectual thinking and for that reason were not at all or only partly comprehensible using complicated approaches. At the time laboratory experi-ments had succeeded only very occasionally, employing mirrors to reflect the sun, in cul-tivating a single daughter blossom from a marigold blossom.

The pendulum was a central tool for her in creating her pictures. Heiny Widmer, who organized the first exhibition of her work in the Kunsthaus of Aargau, Switzerland, in 1973, 10 years after her death, describes how her prints came to be: "Emma Kunz used the pendulum as a stimulus the way other artists use various measures to create favorable conditions for their work. She often said that suddenly an orderly system of dots would turn up in her imagination. She would write them down and interpret them immediately as a basic pattern of a new figure. She then filled out the basic pat-tern, enriched it, consulting her pendulum and inner vision. Often it appeared as though the picture was completed outside her consciousness, as though her hands had been led. When a work was finished, the painter then stood in front of what she found, full of astonishment, returning from the distant depths."[124]

"Having learned the key to this new method of drawing allowed everyone to understand such creations, assuming that they understood numbers." This is what Emma Kunz wrote in her little book *Shaping and Form as Measure, Rhythm, Symbol and Transformation of Number and Principle*. She recognized that her sensitive seeing, feeling, and hearing not only made possible unusual understanding but also could be made visible in pictures of abstract energetic structure.

Perceiving and writing down form interactively was the essence of the artistic work of Emma Kunz (Ill. 204). "The basis for it is the mathematics written in the universe, which she grasped with her pendulum, and over the course of the years she was able to question and to demonstrate this in more and more complex ways," wrote contemporary art journalist Anneliese Zwez when discussing this in her 1988 monograph on Emma Kunz.

"Emma Kunz recognized early on through her work with the pendulum that oscillations are number patterns, and the energy fields of 'crystals, plants, animals and humans' are fluid interplays of the rhythm of numbers," Zwez wrote further. "She calls them the 'power of image of nature', for example in the meaning of Paracelsus, whose work she knew and who said in this sense that everything creates itself anew from the same light, the same energy every day."[125]

The regimented language of words built upon the intellect is too limited to do justice to the work in its entirety. "Something similar takes place when scientists today say that the facts of experimental physics have become too complex to be able to describe them in conventional language," says Harald Szeemann, the independent curator of the Zurich Kunsthaus in Switzerland. The scientist makes use of pictorial symbols, relationship symbols, and formulas in order to be able to make complex relationships visible and plausible.[126]

The well-known Swiss geobiologist Blanche Merz has gone on the search for

Ill. 203: Marigold experiment: 13 daughter blossoms from one mother bloom

Ill. 204: Emma Kunz, Work Nr. 001, 37 x 37 inches (94 x 94 cm). Commentary of Emma Kunz at the creation of her pictures in *Shaping and Form as Measure, Rhythm, Symbol and Transformation of Number and Principle*: "My pictures are meant for the 21st century."

Ill. 203

cryptic picture messages. For Merz, a best-selling author, Emma Kunz is one of the "people with special esoteric knowledge, who from time to time appear in the history of the world in order to advance the spiritual development of mankind." The following is an extensive quotation from Blanche Merz:

"Through her inspired pictures Emma Kunz expressed the interplay of the macrocosm and microcosm and the values inherent in people and possibilities for development in a unique way. In her work her philosophical and scientific knowledge and her cosmic consciousness manifest themselves.

"A century after her birth, Emma Kunz carefully hands us the key to her knowledge of the laws of nature and of all being. This makes possible a first approach to a...higher reality.... The attempt to explain several pictures rests, on the one hand, on fragmentary records from the artist's circle of friends and, on the other hand, on insights which came through intensive examination of the spiritual background of the pictures. In order to grasp the complete power of expression of the works of Emma Kunz we cannot be satisfied with a cursory look. Understanding the themes of the areas of research requires immersing ourselves in the geometrical forms of the depictions of this visionary prophet. The body of her work can bring a message only to the observer open to it.

"...The observation of these many-sided pictures is meant to stimulate the development of spirit and soul—because there are several levels of knowledge. Every person perceives it in his or her own way. The joining of the lines with netting to create forms, shaped by the ancient knowledge of the seer using symbols, fosters a dynamic interaction with the living world. In each work there is an energetic power center, as is also the case in the Mandalas, those abstract picture patterns which are used as aids to meditation; this flows purposefully into the surrounding structures.... Every picture is the expression of a perception which Emma Kunz had experienced internally, created in order to contain answers to, among other things the healing of the soul and body and to reach the delicate spheres of her patients, with the help of the power of her soul and her dynamic aura. Therefore the graphic imitation of works without the personal impulses from Emma Kunz would be a sterile shadow. They would lack the chief basic powers which she sensed.

"The drawings follow a basic framework; for example, the number four. The elements of the drawing are in this case applied four times, connected with the symbol of the material, the physical, the directions of the wind and the seasons. Emma Kunz interprets universal sympathy, the four phases of the moon, the totality of creation with reference to Pythagoras. It is interesting that in the culture of the Celts several graphic analogies of the number four—squares, crosses and stars—are found. But this unusual woman changes the double four structure at the same time to eight, the symbol of infinity. The number eight mediates between the square and the circle, that is, between earth and heaven. In

III. 205

this manner Emma Kunz...found practicable ways to support the development from the earthly to the spiritual.

"...On the trail of today's refined technology you can find from the studies of Erich Neumann that movements of energy necessitating forms result from structures, such as those that were constructed by Emma Kunz. Geometrical forms have an influence on the relationship of electromagnetic powers. These connections between form and energy lead back to the sources, to knowledge about the secrets of nature, to the ability of

III. 205: The moon in the sky above Stonehenge

III. 206: The moon motif visible on earth: according to an Indian prophecy this means a basic change in earth's history.

electromagnetic energies to be guided. The form-related system of radiation in the drawings of Emma Kunz is built upon the same general laws as is the magnetic system of the earth. It results in formation of energy whirlpools, powers which can be guided. The straight lines of column-shaped geometric forms are the simplest and best conductors of energy. It was possible for Emma Kunz, by conscious formation, to allow the form-related energy system to be effective." Blanche Merz is also convinced that several Emma Kunz drawings are documents of concepts "which top modern technology will discover." The seer Emma Kunz predicted the ozone hole and its consequences in 1938, and in 1939 foresaw the development of the atom bomb by Americans. "For that reason the work of Emma Kunz takes on a dimension which points far beyond her person."[127]

The English natural healer and diviner Colin Bloy stated the following at a symposium on the subject of crop circles in England in 1995: "Colored, geometric diagrams will be used as a means of healing in the future. Emma Kunz developed her diagram system, which shows the difference between people of the 20th century and the 21st century."

Another View of Reality

The cosmos was formed according to and upon the basis of laws which are expressed as music, arithmetic and geometry; they bring about harmony, order and balance.
—Edgar Cayce

"Pay attention to the time when you will see signs in the heavens and signs on earth!" This appeal has been heard in various eras and cultures. It speaks of the coming of basic change and a great purification on earth.

"Change" and "purification" can be applied in today's context to global changes in the world around us as well as to our consciousness. The sober observation of our time confirms this. The contemporary world has changed at lightning speed in a single century, bringing more change even than the preceding millennium. And since the middle of the 20th century at the latest, puzzling "signs in the heavens and on earth"

have appeared and are appearing in great numbers. It would be absurd to push aside all of this as "illusion" or "mass psychosis." It at least hints at a change in consciousness among people. Without a doubt, human consciousness is changing at lightning speed. Whether it is in the direction of more reason and wisdom is doubtful, if you consider the condition of the environment as a mirror of human consciousness and action.

Basic damage insurance statistics report sharply rising sums for damage caused by the four elementary forces of fire (fires, volcanoes), water (floods, tidal waves, avalanches), air (hurricanes, tornadoes), earth (earthquakes, landslides), and various combinations of them. In many cases this damage can be directly attributed to the carelessness of people, on the one hand because they provoke catastrophes by thoughtless misuse of the four elements, on the other hand because they expose themselves to dangers through unchecked population growth and development of fragile natural areas. The result is always the same: unending misery.

But is that suffering necessary? Must people learn the hard way, painfully? Could suffering be avoided by better observing the "signs of the times?" These could be the well-known "warning signs" of unleashed elementary forces or the legacy of wise, visionary people such as Emma Kunz or even unusual signs such as lights in the sky or crop circles—no matter how they come about. The British author John Michell, who has dealt extensively with UFOs, prehistoric monuments, and symbolic geometry thinks:

"Without a doubt the psychoanalyst C. G. Jung would have considered crop circles in the same way as these UFOs. For him, they were at the same time carriers and actors of radical changes in the prevailing view of the world. Such changes are apparently necessary."[128]

You no longer need to be a prophet to be able to predict that humanity is on the path to catastrophe if it continues to act as it has in the past century. Even academics speak about this today, unmistakably and in concrete, mathematical terms. But surprisingly our society, which is otherwise always very gullible when it comes to science, is largely ignoring the scientists' warnings. Apparently it is more comfortable to offer up ideals on the altar of growth and stock-market profits.

Undeniably, sweeping changes are taking place with people and their environment at a breathtaking pace. And the fact is that this comes at a time when there is an astrological change from the age of Pisces to that of Aquarius, whether a direct connection is argued or not.

According to many Native American prophecies, people will recognize "when the time of great purification has come" by the appearance of certain signs. It could be argued that crop circles are among these predicted signs. Members of various native tribes speak of a time of change "if you can see the moon in the sky (Ill. 205) and on earth."[129] "Crescent moons" have frequently been a characteristic motif in crop circles (Ill. 206, see also 11, 23, 25, 31, 36, 59, 63, 67, 97, 117, 119, and others).

In the Bible, in Acts 2: 17-19, it is written: "And I will show portents in the heaven above and signs on the earth below.... Your sons and your daughters shall prophesy, and your young men shall see visions, and your old men shall dream dreams." Quite a few Christian people consider the actual appearances of various kinds as the fulfillment of this biblical prophecy.

In a 600-year-old prophecy, the Aztec culture predicts "the end of the consciousness of the 'fifth world' and the beginning of the 'sixth world'": "At the time of the sixth sun everything that was hidden will appear on the earth. Everything which lies hidden under the earth will seek the light of the sun again. Truth will be the seed of life. The sons of the sixth sun will be those who journey among the stars."[130]

For the disciples of the Aztecs as well as of the Maya (see below) a "sun" or "a big sun year" was a period of 26,000 years. In modern astronomy 26,000 years corresponds to the precession. The concept "precession" can be considered the same as movement of the point of spring, caused by movement of the earth's axis, which was discovered by the Greek Hipparchus. Year after year the earth goes through the point of spring and the point of autumn, that is, the points of the equinox, around the sun, at not quite the same place as the previous year, with about 50 seconds difference. As a result, the point of spring moves about 360 degrees in approximately 26,000 years, that is, once in 26,000 years it makes an entire circle. The point of spring moves once through all 12 signs of the zodiac during this time period. Presently the point of spring is moving gradually from Pisces to Aquarius, while the point of autumn is moving gradually from Virgo to Leo.[131]

The total eclipse of the sun on July 11, 1991, above Mexico had a special meaning in the prophecies of the Aztecs. The wise ones of the mysterious Mayan culture, also in Central America, connected this date as well, like the Aztecs, with the "beginning of the sixth sun." Eleven hundred years ago they predicted rapid changes in climate, movements of the earth, and violence connected with political crises for our present time.[132] What has been true in most other countries also has been true in Mexico in recent years; it has been shaken literally by many political changes—civil war and unrest (Chiapas)—and also by natural catastrophes such as floods, drought, volcanic eruptions (Popocatepetl), and earthquakes.

"With the beginning of the sixth sun you will again come into contact with your ancestors from the cosmos," one of the prophecies of the Maya states.[133] It is obvious that many people think of extraterrestrials and UFOs in this connection. The fact is that Mexico is probably the country with the greatest number of and most spectacular UFO sightings in the world (Ills. 180, 182). In 1993, on a clear, nearly smog-free spring day in Mexico City, traffic came to a complete standstill because of such sightings. Even on the Avenida Reforma, a six-lane main artery, amazed people got out of their cars to observe the event in the sky. The daily

III. 207

III. 207: According to an Aztec revelation the time of change has begun when "large animals" appear on the earth. Did they mean animal pictograms (see also Ills. 24, 25, 26, 82, 111, 113, 136)?

papers widely reported the puzzling appearances. But neither the government nor the military said anything about these events, which were filmed hundreds of times. There was little notice taken outside of Mexico, too.

The internationally respected expert on the culture and tradition of Central American peoples, Franzisco Jiminez Sanchez, traveled to England from Mexico in 1996. The spiritual teacher and shaman, better known by the name of Tlakaelel, wanted to visit prehistoric sites and, at the same time, learn more about crop circles. On August 5th, he impressed and touched an audience in southern England with a comprehensive lecture. The forms and symbols of the crop circles, he said, had a connection to the forms and symbols in Mexico, among other places.

For him the symbols included in many crop formations were of great significance.

He was especially impressed by the animal pictograms (III. 207; see also Ills. 18, 24, 25, 26, 82, 111, 113, 136). He pointed to a prophecy of the Aztecs handed down 600 years ago: "Pay attention to the time when the large animals appear on the earth. It will be a time of great change." He stated, when asked who caused the crop circles: "It is cosmic beings. The Hopi Indians have frequent contact with them. They know that they are here and want to bring us further along in our evolutionary process with these signs. They are leading us carefully and are in contact with only a few people."

He especially stressed that another language in addition to the sign language of

the crop circles was important to recognize: "The language of Mother Earth, which speaks to us by means of the elementary powers of fire, water, air, and earth." The earth must make us all the more strongly aware of this where people have forgotten to listen, he said. This language will become clearer in the coming years so that people will find their way back to their connection to the earth. It was used to direct the consciousness on the earth on other paths: "One planet - one humankind. All live in the same house"(see also page 121).

The dreary view of the future foreseen by the Lakota shaman Lame Deer may illustrate just how far away mankind is from this kind of insight: "People have reached a point where they no longer know for what reason they exist. They do not use their brains, and they have forgotten the secret knowledge of their bodies, their senses, and their dreams. They do not use the knowledge that the spirit has given to every individual; they are not even aware of it, and so they stumble blindly on the path to nowhere—on a paved street which they have leveled themselves with bulldozers so that they can reach the big empty hole, which they will find at the end of it and which waits to devour them, sooner. It is a rapid and comfortable highway. But I know where it leads. I have seen it. It was there in my vision, and it makes me shudder if I think of it."

The following simple suggestion from Tlakaelel could show a way out for our restless and helpless spirit: "Everyone should practice care for this planet in his or her own way. The problem is different in different places. But all can create harmony in themselves as the important point of departure for subsequent deeds. In this, intuition, the language of the heart, is of superior meaning. Seek this and act accordingly. Often courage is needed to decide against reason and for the heart. But whoever begins to do that will learn quickly how wise and reliable the language of the heart is."

Even the Englishman John Michell is convinced that crop circles are an expression of suffering nature: "Even if no one has succeeded in explaining the symbols, it is not difficult to understand at least a portion of the message. If nature expresses itself in this way, it is not doing it to offer congratulations.... It cannot be a surprise that many people who are concerned with investigating crop circles are convinced that they are giving us a direct warning.

"The basis for the complaint of nature could lie in the fact that the way of life of modern people today represents a threat for every life on the earth. There are obvious causes such as poisons, environmental pollution, over-exploitation of natural resources and so on. But they do not represent the main cause. For the destructive energies which are at work today proceed...from the predominant scientific-materialistic view of the world on which all modern institutions are founded. It is a partial, incomplete view of the world. For that reason it is unbalanced and its consequences are also. Crop circles represent...a challenge to this view of

Ill. 208

the world. They lead us beyond limitations to a comprehensive, balanced view of reality.

"Nature does not complain in vain, and omens are not only warnings. They also influence people in their attitudes toward putting aside the imbalance that has made the warnings necessary. We are really lucky to live in today's age, in which a process of change from one world view to another is taking place. We are lucky to be witnesses to the signs and wonders which play, as history has told us from time immemorial, a decisive role in this process."[134]

Ill. 208: Remnants of ancient times: a circular island of trees in a sea of grain near Avebury

Ill. 209: The canvas is rolled up. The last crop circles of the year remain only as golden memories. Will they surprise us again next year with new shapes and in new numbers—the crop circles?

Ill. 209

Appendix

Information and Travel Tips

Experience has shown year after year that the most crop circles, by far, appear in southern England. Where and when they will turn up cannot be predicted exactly. But the counties of Wiltshire and Hampshire are regularly the center of activity. In the late 1980s and early 1990s the pubs "the Wagon and the Horse" in Beckhampton and "the Barge Inn" in Alton Barnes served as information exchanges and sources for reports of the latest crop circle appearances.

Today, however, the Internet is the most important and up-to-date source on crop circles and crop circle research. New information is continually posted there, along with aerial photos of the latest crop circles. A list of crop circle websites is on page 143.

Rules of Behavior for Visitors

If you decide to travel to England to investigate the formations firsthand, please—in consideration of farmers, researchers, and others—remember the following when visiting crop circles:

- Ask permission of the farmer or property owner or pay attention to any signs posted. Otherwise there is no right to go onto private property.
- Always use the gate or entryways to enter a field. Do not climb fences. Do not forget to close the gate behind you!
- Vehicles should be parked at parking places outside the field.
- Always approach crop circles on the tractor paths ("tramlines").
- Never go directly through standing grain even if it means you must take long detours.
- Walk carefully within a crop circle to avoid disturbing the plants.
- Do not visit the inner area of a crop circle if it is raining or the field is wet.
- Always stay on the tractor paths.
- Never smoke in a field; there is danger of fire!
- Do not leave any garbage or litter.
- Do not take dogs with you into the fields. If you must, however, always keep the dog on a leash.
- Always respect the property and private living areas of the farmer.

Remember that your behavior will have a lasting influence on the attitudes of farmers and landowners. We all depend on their cooperation. Without it, responsible crop circle research is not possible.

Happy "circling"!

Endnotes

1) Noyes 1990: 18
2) Hesemann 1996: 23-24
3) Thomas 1998: 32-33
4) Hesemann 1996: 14
5) Hesemann 1996: 15
6) Pringle 1999: XI-XIII
7) Thomas 1998: 30
8) Thomas 1998: 30-31
9) Hesemann 1996: 24
10) Thomas 1998:31
11) Hesemann 1996: 25
12) Hesemann 1996: 25, 56
13) Noyes 1990: 31
14) Hesemann 1996: 28
15) Hesemann 1996: 28
16) Hesemann 1996: 28-31
17) Hesemann 1996: 31-32
18) Hesemann 1996: 32
19) Delgado/Andrews 1990: 243-44 (Supplement to *Circular Evidence*)
20) Hesemann 1996: 37
21) Krönig 1992: 144
22) Krönig 1992: Back cover
23) Hesemann 1996: 41
24) Krönig, supplement to *Circular Evidence* 1991: 3
25) Krönig 1992: 218
26) Krönig 1992: 210, 220
27) Krönig 1993: 11
28) Hesemann 1996: 247-48
29) Thomas 1998: 43-46, 86
30) Hesemann 1996: 258
31) Thomas 1998: 46, 86
32) Hesemann 1996: 266
33) Hesemann 1996: 266
34) Video *Das Kornkreis-Phänomen* 1996